RIBBONS
& BOWS

RIBBONS & BOWS

CHRISTINE KINGDOM

~

B.T. BATSFORD LTD.

LONDON

ISBN 0-7134-7496-3

A catalogue record for this book is available from the
British Library

This book was designed and produced by
Quarto Publishing plc
The Old Brewery
6 Blundell Street
London N7 9BH

Senior Editor Cathy Meeus
Copy Editor Christine Parsons
Senior Art Editor Penny Cobb
Designer Debbie Sumner
Assistant Designer Claire Baggaley
Illustrators Sally Launder, Jane Winton, David Kemp
Photographer Paul Forrester
Publishing Director Janet Slingsby
Art Director Moira Clinch

Typeset in Great Britain by Poole Typesetting Ltd,
Bournemouth
Manufactured by Bright Arts (Singapore) Pte Ltd.
Printed by Star Standard Industries (Pte) Ltd.,
Singapore

CONTENTS

INTRODUCTION 6

1 WEAVING 14

Weaving Techniques, Table Mat and Coaster,
Barrel Cushion, Woven-Square Quilt, Wall Organizer

2 RIBBON EMBROIDERY 30

Embroidery Techniques, Picture Frame,
Embroidered Card, Christmas Table Linen,
Make-up Bag, Sampler Panel, Embroidered Cushion

3 PLAITING, PLEATING AND FOLDING ..48

Plaiting and Pleating, Rosettes, Pot Pourri Sachets,
Ribbon-Trimmed Hats

4 APPLIQUÉ AND PATCHWORK..............60

Appliqué and Patchwork Techniques, Trimmed Towels,
Frilled Cushion, Piped Cushion, Log Cabin Quilt,
Appliqué Belts, Evening Bag, Child's Dress and Bag,
Cushion Trims, Curtain Tie-backs

5 BOW-MAKING 80

Bow-Making Techniques, Picture Bow, Gift Wraps,
Christmas Tree Bows, Christmas Basket, Easter Basket

6 ROSE-MAKING 94

Rose-Making Techniques, Festive Table-Centre,
Bridal Head-Dress, Bride's Bouquet, Rose Ball,
Wedding Table-Centre, Rose-Trimmed Parcels

7 CUTTING AND GLUEING 106

Cutting and Glueing, Slotted Cards, Appliqué Cards,
Christmas Garland, Cone Ball, Nut Ring, Spring
Wreath, Ornamental Hat, Decoupage Tray,
Hand-Decorated Ribbons

INDEX 126

CREDITS................................. 128

INTRODUCTION

The very sight of a display of ribbons, glowing with wonderful rich colours and luxurious textures, is enough to fire the imagination. The range of ribbons available today is wider than it has ever been; ribbons have gone far beyond the safe and predictable, and now form a key element of floral, decorative, home furnishings, and clothes trimming crafts.

The use of ribbons, however, is by no means new – there are even Old Testament references to "ribbands". In certain periods of history, ribbons were the subject of legislation – only the nobility were allowed to wear them – but by the 17th century they had become popular for everyone, and the lavish use of ribbon - decorated clothing became a status symbol. Men's clothing from that period could be embellished with as much as 250 metres of ribbon.

The Victorians, too, loved to use ribbons, both on clothing and on home furnishings, and it was they who invented some of the ribbon-crafts that are enjoying such a popular revival today, such

Ribbon projects made in Victorian colours can create a sumptuous, traditional look.

Bring the freshness of the garden into your home with wreaths and baskets decorated with ribbons and flowers.

*Ribbons in jazzy
colours are perfect
for making
furnishing trims to
complement a
modern home.*

*Ribbon roses in
satins and sheers
are ideal for
creating romantic
wedding accessories
and gift wraps.*

as
ribbon
embroi-
dery and
weaving.
You'll find
these traditional
crafts in Ribbons and Bows,
but you'll also find a great many
more modern ideas, made possible by the
technical advances in the manufacture of ribbons. You'll discover how to add style and colour
to flower arrangements by adding bows and
loops, how to trim hats, garments and
Christmas wrappings with pretty ribbon roses or rosettes, how to make ribbon patchwork or appliqué designs
for a bedspread or cushion cover, and
how to use craft ribbon for a series of
delightful greetings cards.

Ribbon-crafts are great fun, and
quick to do – ideal for our busy
lifestyles. And best of all, most of
them need little or no sewing
skill.. Whether you are
gifted with nimble fingers,
or are one of those who is
"all thumbs", you will find
projects in the book to
suit your needs – even if
you have only a short time
to spare for craft work.

The ribbons themselves will
also suit any needs, allowing you to be as

individual as you like in your choice of colours and styles without sacrificing practicality.

They are available in every possible finish, colour and pattern, and in widths ranging from as narrow as 1.5mm (1/16 in) to as wide as 80mm (3in). The information on the next few pages will give you some idea of the variety of ribbons at your disposal, and if you need further inspiration, visit a store and see them laid out in all their glory.

CRAFT RIBBONS

Also referred to as cut-edge or florist's ribbons, these are created by cutting large rolls of fabric lengthwise into strips of the desired width. A special finish adds crispness and keeps the fabric from fraying. Because of this finish, craft ribbons are normally not washable, but some can be dry cleaned, so check the manufacturer's instructions before using them on clothes or home furnishings.

Hand-made Christmas accessories and gifts in reds and greens provide a wonderful opportunity to use ribbon-craft skills.

WIRE-EDGED CRAFT RIBBONS

These are made by fusing a wire along the edges of cut-edge craft ribbon or by fusing wire into seams made by turning over the raw edges of the ribbon. These methods are suitable only for some relatively plain weaves.

Wire-edged craft ribbon

MERROWED CRAFT RIBBON

This is made with a close satin stitch that produces a fine finished edge. Most merrowed ribbons

Wire-edged taffeta

are wired, the wire having been fused or held along the ribbon edge as the stitching takes place. The most common threads used for merrowing are glazed cotton or metallic.

WOVEN-EDGE RIBBONS

Wire-edged woven

These are essentially narrow pieces of fabric with two selvage edges. Although a few are dry-clean-only, the majority are washable, making them ideal for any type of clothing or home furnishings project. Woven-edged ribbons are available in a wide variety of types.

WIRE-EDGED WOVEN

A thin, flexible wire is woven along each edge during the manufacture. Wire-edge ribbons have exciting possibilities for shaped bows and roses, as they retain their shape indefinitely. Roses are easy to make by gathering up one of the wires like a pull-cord, or the wires can be pulled out altogether, allowing you to combine the crisp wired ribbon with soft, fluid streamers and appliquéd ribbons.

Grosgrain

GROSGRAIN

These ribbons, which are crisp and stable, have a distinctive crosswise rib. They are available in solid colours, patterns and stripes. Stripes are generally woven in and patterns are printed on. There are some interesting variations such as a ribbon with satin edges and a grosgrain centre.

SATIN

Soft, supple and easy to handle. Singleface satins have one shiny and

Singleface satin

Singleface satin

one dull side, while doubleface are shiny on both sides and are a bit thicker than singleface. Doubleface ribbons are almost always plain, but single face ribbons can be printed with a pattern, generally on one side only. Special effects include picot or feather-edge, metallic edges or a grosgrain centre panel with satin borders.

Moiré taffeta

Jacquards

JACQUARDS

Woven ribbons with a tapestry effect. Florals, small geometrics and ethnic patterning are the most common motifs.

TAFFETA

Very finely woven and available in both solid colours and prints, but most familiar as stripes, plaids and checks. When the design is woven in, the ribbon is the same on both sides. The overall effect of most taffetas is matt rather than shiny.

MOIRÉ TAFFETA

Crisp and elegant, with a shimmering, watermark finish, this ribbon is well suited for making bows.

Ombré taffeta

Checked taffeta

SHEER

Ideal for light, airy embellishments, such as loops and bows. Sheers can be printed or plain, and some have satin or metallic stripes woven into the sheer. Many sheers are made with a monofilament edge which is an integral part of the ribbon.

MONOFILAMENT-EDGE

The monofilaments are along the edges and actually function as thicker lengthwise threads that are an integral part of the ribbon's construction and cannot be removed. They are normally used for sheers or ribbons made from very fine fibres. Bows fashioned from this ribbon have a crisp appearance, but the ribbon is also soft enough to be applied to a garment.

Satin-edge sheer

METALLIC

Made from lurex and similar metallic fibres, and sometimes interwoven with another fibre, these ribbons are perfect for evening wear and festive decorations. Iridescents are also used to create pearlized effects.

Metallic

Monofilament-edge sheer

VELVET

These ribbons have a plush pile, giving both deep, rich colours and solid substance.

Velvet

PREGATHERED

Gathered along one edge, these are ideal for quick finishes on clothing and home decor items.

PLEATED

Knife- or box-pleated and often stitched along one edge, these can create a unique effect on both clothing and home furnishings.

EMBELLISHED

Enhanced by adding pearls or lace, embellished ribbons are popular for bridal and special occasion dressing. The base ribbon is usually, but not always, a single face satin.

RIBBON WIDTH

Ribbons are available in a variety of widths, expressed in inches or millimetres. Consult the chart right when checking ribbon widths.

Ribbons are sold both by the metre (or yard) and in prepacked lengths. In addition, ready-made ribbon roses and bows are available in everything from sheers to satins to metallics. These can be useful, and guarantee uniform size and shape.

CONVERSION CHART	
Ribbon Width	
1.5mm	$^1/_{16}$ in
3mm	$^1/_8$ in
5mm	$^3/_{16}$ in
7mm	$^1/_4$ in
9mm	$^3/_8$ in
12mm	$^1/_2$ in
15mm	$^5/_8$ in
23mm	$^7/_8$ in
39mm	1 $^1/_2$ in
56mm	2 $^1/_4$ in
77mm	3 in

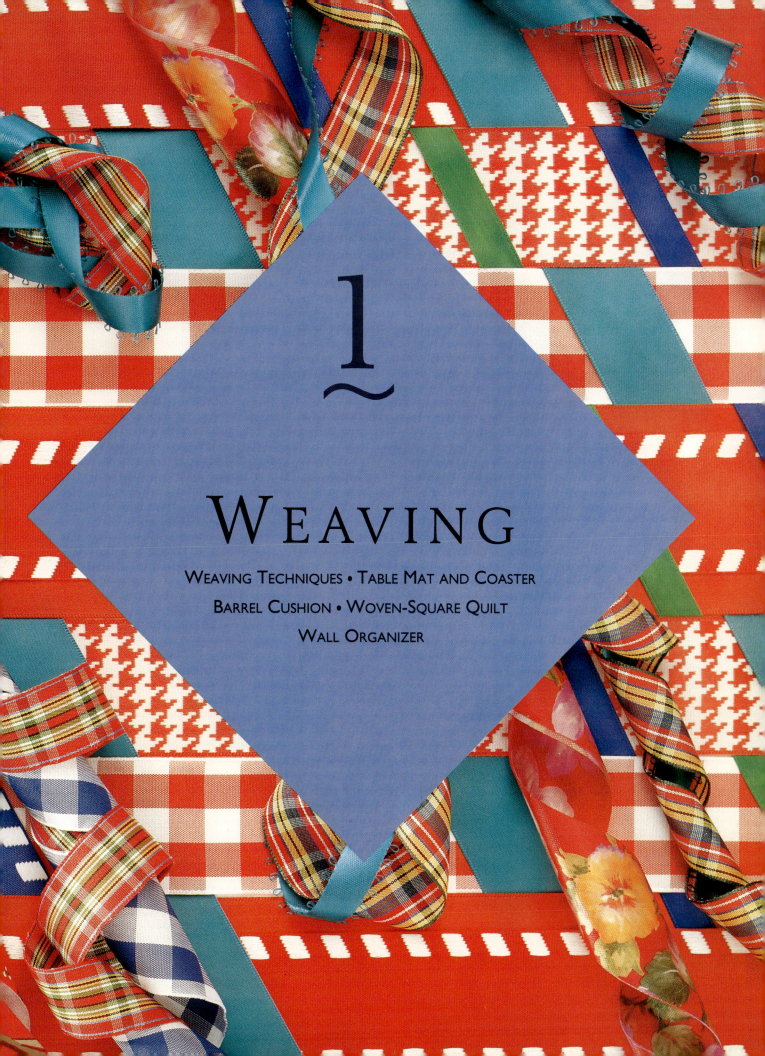

1
~

WEAVING

WEAVING TECHNIQUES • TABLE MAT AND COASTER

BARREL CUSHION • WOVEN-SQUARE QUILT

WALL ORGANIZER

WEAVING TECHNIQUES

Ribbon weaving is one of the simplest needlecrafts to learn. No special equipment or tools are necessary – most can be found around the home or in the sewing basket.

Most ribbon weaving comprises three stages: preparing the interfacing; weaving the ribbon; and bonding the ribbon. The first and last stages are the same for all weaving. For all weaving patterns remember that the term "warp" refers to the vertical ribbons and "weft" to the horizontal ribbons.

PREPARING THE INTERFACING

2.5cm (1in) ►

1 Draw a square of the required dimensions adding a 2.5cm (1in) seam allowance all round.
2 With the adhesive side up, pin the interfacing at its corners onto the pin board. You can now proceed with the weaving.

BONDING THE RIBBONS

1 When you have completed your weave, lightly press the ribbons to bond them onto the interfacing, using a dry iron on a moderate set-ting. Having angled the pins away from the work, you should be able to press the ribbons at the outer edge with the tip of the iron.
2 When you are sure all the ribbons are held in place, remove all the pins, turn the weaving over and with a moderately hot steam setting (or a damp cloth and moderately hot iron) press the ribbons securely in place. Allow the weaving to cool thoroughly before making it up into your chosen article.

MATERIALS

- Pin board large enough for the piece of weaving
- Glass headed pins
- Scissors
- Steam iron (or a dry iron and damp cloth)
- Lightweight iron-on interfacing
- Pencil/ballpoint-pen, ruler, tape-measure
- Safety pin
- Ribbon (see Estimating ribbon quantities)

ESTIMATING RIBBON QUANTITIES

This chart gives the approximate quantities of ribbons needed for weaves without a diagonal weave using the same width of ribbon throughout. If you want to use different colours, divide the total length of ribbon required between the colours. The chart gives the length of ribbons required in metres (yards), including a 2.5cm (1in) seam allowance, for various sizes of woven squares.

People tend to weave with varying tensions so the quantities given above are only estimated amounts. You may find that you use a little less than those shown if you work with a 'loose' tension.

WIDTH OF RIBBON	SIZE OF SQUARE		
	10cm (4in)	20cm (8in)	30cm (12in)
5mm (³⁄₁₆in)	6 (6½)	20 (22)	42 (45½)
7mm (¼in)	4.2 (4½)	14.6 (15¾)	30.2 (32¾)
9mm (³⁄₈in)	3.4 (3½)	11 (12)	23.2 (25)
15mm (⅝in)	2.2 (2¼)	6.6 (7)	14 (15¼)
23mm (⅞in)	1.2 (1½in)	4.6 (5)	9.2 (10)

PLAIN WEAVE

To make a simple 30cm (12in) square in plain weave you will need:

    4.60m (5yd) of 23mm (⅞in) ribbon in a light colour

    4.60m (5yd) of 23mm (⅞in) ribbon in a dark colour

    35cm (14in) square of interfacing

1 Prepare the interfacing as described opposite. Cut the warp (vertical) ribbons into 35cm (14in) lengths

2 Pin these ribbons vertically from the top edge of the interfacing starting at the left-hand seam line. The ribbons should just be touching each other, but not overlapping. Angle the pins away from the work as this helps at the bonding stage.

Weaving is an ideal technique for making cushion covers. This cushion in soft pastel colours uses plain weave.

3 Cut the weft (horizontal) ribbon into the 35cm (14in) required lengths.

4 With a safety pin in one end, weave the first weft ribbon through the warp ribbons, over the first, under the second, over the third and so on until finally over the last ribbon. You can work either from left to right or right to left.

5 Push this first weft ribbon up to top seam line. Ensure it is straight and taut, pin it down at each end and remove the safety pin.

6 Take the second weft ribbon and weave it through the warp ribbons, this time under the first, over the second, under the third, and so on.

7 Push this ribbon up as close as possible to the first weft ribbon, ensuring it is straight and taut, then pin in position.

8 Continue weaving the remaining ribbons until you have completed all weft ribbons. Then bond the ribbons to the interfacing as described opposite.

Note You may find that your last ribbon has gone over the bottom seam line. If it is by only a small amount, do not worry as this is normal, but if it is more than 1cm (½in) either push the weft ribbons closer together, or discard the last ribbon.

ZIG-ZAG WEAVE

This weave works best with ribbons in just two different colours, although you can vary the effect by using different widths.

RIBBON QUANTITIES

To make a simple 30cm (12in) square in zig-zag weave you will need:

    15.40m (16¾yd) of 7mm (¼in) ribbon colour A

    14.70m (16yd) of 7mm (¼in) ribbon colour B

    35cm (14in) square of interfacing

1 After preparing the interfacing as described on page 16, cut all the ribbon into 35cm (14in) lengths.

2 Starting at the left-hand seam line, pin alternate coloured warp ribbons from the top edge of the interfacing. Start and finish with colour A.

3 Starting at the top border drawn on the interfacing, weave the weft ribbons as follows:

    ROW 1 Colour A *Over 2, under 2, and so on to the end.*

    ROW 2 Colour B *Under 1, over 2, under 2, over 2 and so on in twos to the end.*

    ROW 3 Colour A *Under 2, over 2, under 2, and so on in twos to the end.*

    ROW 4 Colour B *Over 1, under 2, over 2, under 2, and so on in twos to the end. Repeat this sequence until you have completed your square.*

4 Bond the ribbon weaving to the interfacing as described on page 16.

Zig-zag weave produces an immediate impact whether woven with ribbons of contrasting or toning colours.

PATCHWORK WEAVE

Interesting patchwork effects are easy to work and you will discover many ways of creating patchwork squares as you become more adventurous. The following design uses ribbons in three different colours.

RIBBON QUANTITIES

To make a simple 30cm (12in) square in patchwork weave you will need:

    15m (16¼yd) of 7mm (¼in) ribbon colour A

    7m (7½yd) of 7mm (¼in) ribbon colour B

    7m (7½yd) of 7mm (¼in) ribbon colour C

    35cm (14in) square of interfacing

1 After preparing the interfacing as described on page 16, cut all the ribbon into 35cm (14in) lengths.

2 Starting at the left-hand seam line pin the warp ribbons from the top edge of the interfacing in the following sequence of colours:

ABAC/A/CABA.

Depending on the size of the piece you are working, you can add extra sequences of "ABAC" and "CABA" on each side of the central "A", which will maintain the symmetrical pattern.

3 Starting at the top seam line drawn on the interfacing, weave the weft ribbons in the same colour sequence as above:

ROW 1 Colour A *Under 1, and then over 2, under 2, over 2 and so on in twos.*

ROW 2 Colour B *Under 1, over 1, under 1, over 1, and so on until the end.*

ROW 3 Colour A *Over 2, under 2, over 2, under 2, and so on until the end.*

ROW 4 Colour C *Over 1, and then under 1, over 3, under 1, over 3, under 1, over 3, and so on until the end.*

4 Repeat this sequence down to the bottom seam line. You may have a few ribbons left over.

5 Bond the ribbon weaving to the interfacing as described on page 16.

TUMBLING BLOCKS
WEAVE

This is an exciting weave with its optical illusion enhanced by a careful choice of ribbons. It is made with the usual warp and weft ribbons plus a third narrower diagonal ribbon. The final result depends entirely on the colour of the ribbons you choose.

RIBBON QUANTITIES
To make a simple 30cm (12in) square you will need:

4.60m (5yd) of 23mm (⅞in) ribbon in a light colour for the warp

4.60m (5yd) of 23mm (⅞in) ribbon in a medium colour the weft

7.60m (8¼yd) of 15mm (⅝in) ribbon in a dark colour for the diagonal weave.

35cm (14in) square of interfacing

1 After preparing the interfacing as described on page 16, cut only the warp and weft ribbons into 35cm (14in) lengths – 13 of each colour.

2 Starting at the left-hand seam line, pin the 13 warp ribbons from the top edge of the interfacing, with the ribbons just touching each other but not overlapping.

3 Starting at the top seam line weave the weft ribbons as follows:

ROW 1 *Under 1, then over 1, under 2, over 1, under 2 and so on to the end.*

ROW 2 *Over 1, under 2, over 1, under 2 and so on to the end.*

ROW 3 *Under 2, over 1, under 2, over 1, and so on to the end.*

Repeat this sequence for the remain-

Inspired by traditional quilt designs, patchwork weave, seen here made up into a cushion cover, allows you to use three different colours of ribbon.

ing ribbons, weaving them very closely together, touching if possible.

4 Prepare to weave the diagonal ribbon working from bottom right up through to top left. You might find it a help to use a safety pin on the end of the ribbon to feed it through.

Note: It may be necessary temporarily to remove a pin holding down a weft or warp ribbon as you thread the diagonal ribbon through, but don't forget to put it back before going on to the next diagonal.

5 Begin to weave the diagonal as follows: starting from bottom right edge, feed the diagonal ribbon over the first and second warp ribbons and under the second weft ribbon. Feed the ribbon back out again from above the third weft ribbon where it crosses the fourth warp ribbon.

6 Feed the ribbon back under the fifth warp ribbon where it goes over the next weft ribbon and back out from under the next weft ribbon where it goes over the next-but-on warp.

7 Continue feeding the diagonal ribbon through the weave in this sequence until the ribbon emerges at the top left corner of the work. Pull the diagonal ribbon over the final warp and onto the seam allowance. Pin it down. Make sure the diagonal is straight and taut, then pin down the other end and cut it to length.

8 Continue weaving in the diago-

nals above the one you have just done in the following sequence: in under a weft and out from under the next weft up but two warps across. Then under the weft two above and one warp along.

9 Next, weave in the diagonals below the first one in the same way. When all the diagonal ribbons have been woven, smooth down the whole piece with your hand, repositioning some of the pins if necessary. Fuse the ribbon weaving to the interfacing as described on page 16.

Note: When weaving the Tumbling Blocks within a rectangle, the diagonal ribbons do not follow the true diagonals of the rectangle but start at one corner and eventually emerge off-set in the opposite corner.

The fresh summery fragrance of lavender captured in woven ribbon! Eleven supple lavender stems are tied together under the flowerheads with a 2m (6ft) length of 3mm ribbon. Bend the stalks back on themselves and weave the ribbon in and out. Leave in a warm place to dry, then draw up, tighten and secure the ribbon. Trim with dried flowers and bows.

TABLE MAT AND COASTER

*As these mats should be washable, choose good quality
ribbons that can withstand frequent washing, and will also
easily shed the occasional food or wine stain.*

MATERIALS

Ribbons
- 8.50m (9¼yd) of 39mm (1½in) wide
  taffeta tartan
- 1.50m (1¾yd) of 23mm (⅞in) wide
  taffeta tartan

Other materials
- For mat: 35cm by 50cm (14in by
  20in) piece of washable backing
  fabric, and same size in medium
  weight iron-on interfacing
- For coaster: 14cm (5½in) square of
  washable backing fabric, and same in
  interfacing, as above
- 2.50m (3yd) of bias binding

THE MAT

1 Following the plain weave instructions (page 17), weave a rectangle using twelve 35cm (14in) lengths of 39mm (1½in) wide ribbon as the warp and five 50cm (20in) lengths of the 39mm (1½in) ribbon as the weft.

2 Tack the panel and backing together on right side, then round off the corners.

3 Open out one edge of the bias binding and then machine stitch it around the edges of the mat, overlapping the ends for a neat join.

4 Turn binding to wrong side, and hand stitch edge along line of machine stitching.

THE COASTER

Make exactly as above using five 14cm (5½in) lengths of the 23mm (⅞in) ribbon for both the warp and the weft.

BARREL CUSHION

This cushion uses ribbons in a variety of ways. The zig-zag weave is most prominent, with plaited trims and rosettes to finish off the ends.

MATERIALS

Ribbons – all single faced satin
- 17m (18½yd) of 7mm (¼in) wide cream
- 17m (18½yd) of 7mm (¼in) wide tan
- 1.20m (1½yd) of 9mm (⅜in) wide featheredge cream
- 1.50m (1¾yd) of 9mm (⅜in) wide tan
- 4m (4½yd) of 1.5mm (⅟₁₆in) wide cream
- 7.10m (7¾yd) of 23mm (⅞in) wide tan
- 1.50m (1¾yd) of 3mm (⅛in) wide tan

Other materials
- Barrel cushion pad 46cm (18in) long and 19cm (7½in) in diameter
- Mustard cotton drill fabric 70cm (28in) square for cushion cover and rosettes
- Fine iron-on interfacing 23cm by 67cm (9in by 27in)
- Buckram 16cm (6½in) square

WEAVING

Prepare a piece of zig-zag weave 18cm by 62cm (7in by 24½in) using the 17m (18½yd) of cream and tan 7mm (¼in) wide ribbon. Trim off ribbon ends and interfacing to leave a 1cm (½in) border around the weave.

MAKING UP THE CUSHION COVER

■ From fabric cut a piece 70cm by 62cm (28in by 24½in). With right sides facing, pin, tack and machine zig-zag the woven panel centrally across the fabric. To hide the raw edges, machine a length of 23mm (⅞in) tan ribbon down each 62cm (24½in) long edge, stitching down both sides of each ribbon.

Scale I square = 4cm (1½in)

2 Cut the 4m (4½yd) of 1.5mm (¹⁄₁₆in) wide ribbon into three equal lengths and plait together as described on page 50. Cut the plait into two equal lengths, then hand sew each one to the outer edges of the 23mm (⅞in) ribbon.

3 Approximately 5cm (2in) along from both lengths of plaiting, machine two rows of 23mm (⅞in) wide ribbon, butting the edges together, then machine one row of 9mm (⅜in) featheredge ribbon centrally over the butted edges.

4 Right side facing, fold the fabric in half, pin, tack and machine together along the 70cm (28in) raw edge with a 1.5cm (½in) wide seam. Make a narrow casing in each end as shown, leaving a small gap in the stitching; thread a draw-string of 9mm (⅜in) plain ribbon through.

5 Insert the cushion pad into the cover, pull up the draw-strings and fasten in a bow.

THE ROSETTES

Make up two petal rosettes using the remaining 23mm (⅞in) tan ribbon, 1.50m (1¾yd) of 3mm (⅛in) ribbon, the remaining cushion fabric and two 6cm diameter circles of buckram.

Handstitch the rosettes in place at the ends of the cushion so they can easily be unpicked and replaced before and after washing.

MAKING THE ROSETTES

1 Cover buckram with fabric to make centre medallion. Turn to wrong side and stitch close to edge. Trim excess fabric.

2 Make 14 petal points from 12cm (4½in) lengths of 23mm ribbon.

3 Place in a spiral on the wrong side of the medallion. Stitch or bond to secure at centre.

4 Cut the 3mm (⅛in) ribbon into three equal lengths and make a simple plait (see page 50). Press and stitch around edge of medallion, folding raw edges of plait to wrong side. Stitch to secure and trim excess.

Woven-square quilt

The quilt has a total of 13 plain weave squares, and uses soft, natural tones and different ribbon widths to create a very elegant effect.

MATERIALS

Ribbons
- 5m (5½yd) of 9mm (⅜in) wide cream
- 8.50m (9¼yd) of 7mm (¼in) wide maize
- 9.60m (10½yd) of 15mm (⅝in) wide maize
- 4m (4½yd) of 15mm (⅝in) wide corn
- 28.80m (31¼yd) of 15mm (⅝in) wide toffee brown
- 9.60m (10½yd) of 3mm (⅛in) wide rust
- 18.80m (20½yd) of 15mm (⅝in) wide pale brown
- 19.20m (21yd) of 15mm (⅝in) wide moss green
- 5.10m (5½yd) of 23mm (⅞in) wide stone
- 1.50m (1¾yd) of 9mm (⅜in) wide featheredge stone
- 10.50m (11½yd) of 9mm (⅜in) wide toffee brown

Other materials
- 2.90m (3¼yd) of pale rust coloured closely woven cotton 137cm (54in) wide
- 1.35m (1½yd) of 90cm (36in) wide fine iron-on interfacing
- 120cm (47in) square of 12oz polyester wadding

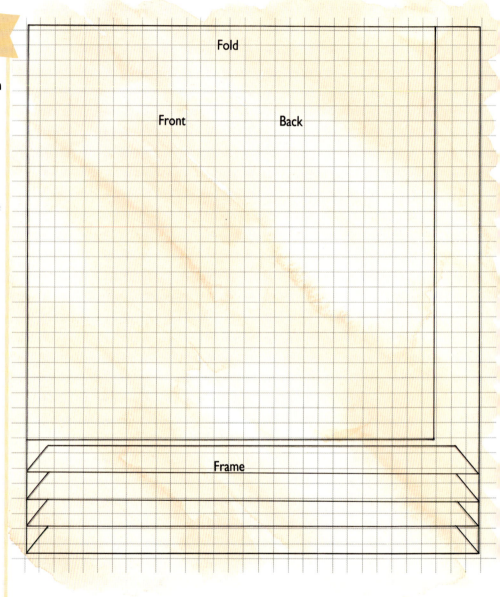

Scale 1 square = 4cm (1½in)

WEAVING THE SQUARES

Following the plain weave instructions (page 17) weave thirteen (finished size) 22cm (9in) squares. There are four different patterns.

PATTERN 1 SQUARES

PATTERN 3 SQUARES

PATTERN 2 SQUARES

1 Weave four pattern 1 squares using the following ribbons: 9mm (⅜in) cream, 15mm (⅝in) corn and the 7mm (¼in) and 15mm (⅝in) maize.

2 Pin the warp ribbons: one cream, thirteen corn, one cream.

3 Weave the weft ribbons: one cream and then alternately using ten of the 15mm (⅝in) and nine of the 7mm (¼in) maize and finally one cream.

1 Weave four, using the following ribbons: 15mm (⅝in) toffee brown, 3mm (⅛in) rust and 15mm (⅝in) pale brown.

2 Pin the warp ribbons as follows: toffee brown, rust, toffee brown, rust, toffee brown, seven pale brown, toffee brown, rust, toffee brown, rust, toffee brown. Weave the weft ribbons in the same order.

1 Weave four using the following ribbons: 15mm (⅝in) moss green and 15mm (⅝in) pale brown.

2 Pin the warp ribbons: three pale brown, eight moss green, three pale brown.

3 Weave the weft ribbons in the same order as the warp ribbons.

PATTERN 4 SQUARES

1 Weave one pattern 4 square using the following ribbons: 23mm (⅞in) stone and 9mm (⅜in) featheredge stone.

2 Pin ten of the 23mm (⅞in) stone for the warp ribbons.

3 Weave the weft ribbons: alternately seven of the 23mm (⅞in) stone with six of the 9mm (⅜in) featheredge stone.

4 When all the squares have been completed, trim back the ribbon ends and interfacing to leave a 1cm (½in) seam allowance around each 22cm (9in) square of weaving.

MAKING UP THE QUILT

1 Cut two 127cm (50in) squares from the fabric.

2 Take one fabric square (the top) and starting 5cm (2in) in from one edge mark a further five points at 22cm (9in) intervals along the top and bottom edges and down the two sides. Using these points as guides fold the fabric across in straight lines and lightly press to form a grid to mark the positions of the woven squares.

3 Pin, tack and machine with a zig-zag stitch the woven squares to the right side of the top fabric as shown.

4 Cut the 9mm (⅜in) toffee brown edging ribbon into eight equal lengths. Pin, tack and machine the lengths in place as shown, stitching down along both the ribbon edges to cover the raw edges of the weaving.

5 With wrong sides together, sandwich the wadding between the top and bottom pieces of fabric. Tack together through all thicknesses around the edges.

6 From remaining fabric, cut eight strips each 137cm (54in) by 7cm (3in) for the border. Mitre the ends at 45 degrees as shown.

7 Wrong sides facing, pin and machine each set of four strips together across the mitred ends to form two frames. Turn to right side and trim away excess at corners.

8 Press under 1.5cm (½in) on inside edges of both frames to wrong side. Right sides facing outward, position one frame on right side of quilt, with outer edge 2cm (¾in) outside that of the quilt. Pin, tack and machine close to inside edge of frame.

9 Place second frame on top of first, right sides together, and matching borders together at outside edges. Machine stitch a 1cm (⅜in) seam around, clip seam allowance across the corners, turn border through to right side, and handstitch inside edge of border to wrong side of quilt.

WALL ORGANIZER

Brightly coloured and cleverly designed, this useful organizer is a brilliant store-all for baby's changing needs, toddler's toys, or for a teenager's bedroom.

Ribbons
- 2.80m (3yd) of 39mm (1½in) wide star print
- 10.50m (11½yd) of 9mm (⅜in) wide jade
- 3.50m (4yd) of 9mm (⅜in) wide blue spot
- 3m (3¼yd) of 9mm (⅜in) wide pink
- 6.80m (7½yd) of 9mm (⅜in) wide pink spot
- 10m (11yd) of 9mm (⅜in) wide blue
- 5.70m (6¼yd) of 3mm (⅛in) wide yellow
- 4m (4¼yd) of 3mm (⅛in) wide blue
- 2.80m (3yd) of 3mm (⅛in) wide jade

Other materials
- Heavy duty interfacing 100cm by 56cm (40in by 22in)
- 2.60m (3yd) of 112cm (44in) wide blue cotton gaberdine
- 60cm (24in) of 90cm (36in) wide medium weight iron-on interfacing
- 75cm (30in) length of 19mm (¾in) wooden dowel

Note In this project, medium weight iron-on interfacing is suggested for both the weaving and the stiffening of the pockets.

WEAVING

Following the instructions for plain weave (page 17), and referring to the diagram on page 29 for the position of the pockets, weave the pocket fabric.

K E Y

A = Pocket A
B = Pocket B
C = Pocket C
D = Pocket D
E = Pocket E
F = Edge Binding
G = Loops
H = Front and back pieces

Scale I square = 4cm (1½in)

POCKET A

Plain weave 19.5cm by 27cm (8in by 10½in) using 7mm (¼in) jade and pink and 9mm (⅜in) wide blue spot ribbon.

1 Pin the warp ribbons along the 19.5cm (8in) top edge as follows: three jade, three blue spot, one pink, four jade, two pink, four jade, one pink, three blue spot, three jade.

2 Weave the warp ribbons down the 27cm (10½in) length as follows: three jade, three blue spot, one pink, four jade, four pink, four jade, one pink, three blue spot, three jade.

POCKET B

Make two pieces of plain weave 10cm by 15cm (4in by 6in) using 9mm (⅜in) pink spot and blue and 3mm (⅛in) yellow.

1 Pin the warp ribbons along the 10cm (4in) top edge: three pink spot, blue, yellow, blue, yellow, blue, three pink spot.

2 Weave the weft ribbons down the 15cm (6in) length: five pink spot, blue, yellow, blue, yellow, blue, five pink spot.

POCKET C

Plain weave 10cm by 15cm (4in by 6in) using 9mm (⅜in) blue, 7mm (¼in) jade and 3mm (⅛in) yellow.

1 Pin the warp ribbons along the 10cm (4in) top edge: two yellow, eight blue, two yellow.

2 Weave the weft ribbons down the 15cm (6in) length: two yellow, fifteen jade, two yellow.

POCKETS D AND E

Make four pieces of basic weave each 5cm by 8.5cm (2in by 3½in). Weave two pockets D using 3mm (⅛in) yellow, blue and jade in the weaving pattern of Pocket C.

Pockets E use 9mm (⅜in) pink spot and 3mm (⅛in) pink, yellow and blue.

1 Pin the warp ribbons along the 5cm (2in) top edge: pink, pink spot, pink, blue, yellow, blue, yellow, blue, pink, pink spot, pink.

2 Weave the weft ribbons down the 8.5cm (3½in) length: pink spot, pink, pink spot, pink, blue, yellow, blue, yellow, blue, pink, pink spot, pink, pink spot.

When all the weaving has been completed trim off the ribbon ends and interfacing to leave just under 1cm (⅜in) border all around the interwoven shapes.

CONSTRUCTING THE POCKETS

1 Following the diagrams, draw and cut out the pocket patterns on paper and then in fabric and interfacing as follows. Each pocket has two fabric pieces, one for the outside and one for the inside. Cut out pocket A twice in fabric and once in iron-on interfacing. Cut out pockets B and C a total of six times in fabric and three in iron-on interfacing. Cut out pockets D and E eight times in fabric and four in iron-on interfacing

2 Iron the interfacing onto wrong side of outside pocket pieces.

3 Machine the woven panels to the

right sides of the pocket fronts. To cover the raw edges, machine on lengths of 9mm (⅜in) blue ribbon.

4 Right sides together, seam pocket fronts and backs. Turn to right side and press.

5 On inside, stitch together the right-angled lower edges of pockets A, B and C to form a box shape.

6 Turn to right side and machine stitch close to edges.

FIXING THE POCKETS IN PLACE

1 Following diagram, draw in the positions of the pockets on the heavy duty interfacing.

2 Lay the interfacing on the fabric and cut two pieces 1cm (⅜in) larger all round for a seam allowance. Stitching around the edges, tack the

interfacing to the wrong side of one piece of fabric (markings outermost). With a length of contrast-colour thread, tack along all the pocket positions so they show clearly on the right side of the fabric.

3 Using this tacking as a guide, machine the side edges of the small pockets D and E in place. Machine the 39mm (1½in) star ribbon across the width of the organizer to cover the raw edges at the bottom edges of the pockets.

4 Turn in and press 1cm (⅜in) to wrong side on both open (bottom) edges of pocket A. Position and machine this edge in place, then machine side edges in place.

5 Stitch the top three pockets B and C in place in the same way as pocket A.

6 Machine a length of 39mm (1½in) star ribbon just under the top three pockets.

COMPLETING THE ORGANIZER

1 With wrong sides together, tack the backing and front fabrics together, sandwiching the interfacing in between.

2 For the hanging loops cut three pieces of 39mm (1½in) star ribbon, each 22cm (9in) long. From fabric, cut three pieces 6cm by 22cm (2½in by 9in). Turn in 1cm (⅜in) to wrong side down each long edge and press. Wrong sides together, lay ribbons on top and machine close to side edges. Fold each loop in half and tack in place.

3 From remaining fabric, cut two strips 100cm by 4cm (40in by 1½in) wide, and two 60cm by 4cm (24in by 1½in). Use these to bind the edges of the organizer, covering the sides first.

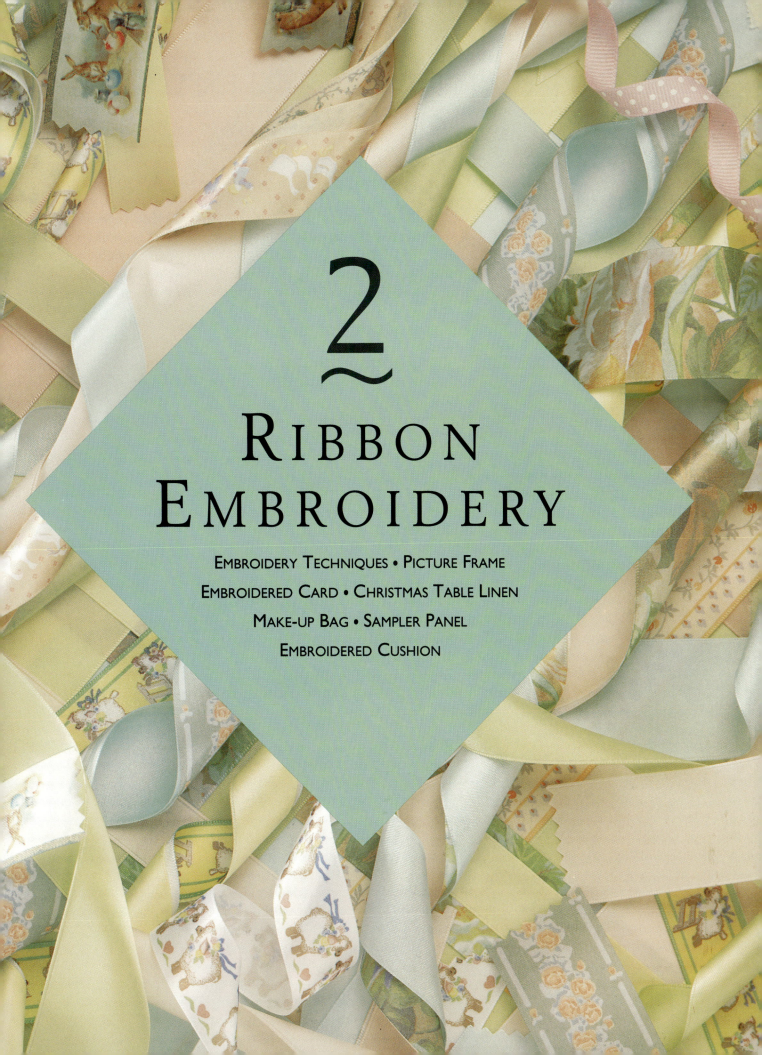

2
~
RIBBON EMBROIDERY

EMBROIDERY TECHNIQUES • PICTURE FRAME

EMBROIDERED CARD • CHRISTMAS TABLE LINEN

MAKE-UP BAG • SAMPLER PANEL

EMBROIDERED CUSHION

EMBROIDERY TECHNIQUES

One of the oldest ribbon craft techniques, this free-style decoration uses narrow ribbons in the same way as embroidery thread.

1 Hold the ribbon flat against the fabric under your left thumb while you take a stitch.

STARTING AND FINISHING

Start your first stitch by making a tiny backstitch to secure the ribbon. As a finishing stitch, knotting the ribbon creates too much bulk at the back of the work and the ribbon may come undone, so weave the ribbon behind the stitching, or leave a tail to be caught by the next stitch.

KEEPING THE RIBBON FLAT

For most kinds of embroidery it is important to keep the ribbon flat. It helps if you keep ribbon lengths short, about 30cm (12in), as it is easier to see and remove twists.

2 Keep your thumb in place while you tighten the ribbon firmly over it. In most cases this will remove twists before the stitch is completed. If you do need to adjust a stitch, carefully use a round ended tapestry needle to loosen the ribbon.

STITCHES

The projects on the following pages use a variety of stitches, each of which is illustrated here.

FEATHER STITCH

DOUBLE FEATHER STITCH

HERRINGBONE STITCH

CHAIN STITCH

STEM STITCH

FLY STITCH

LAZY DAISY STITCH

FRENCH KNOT

CRETAN STITCH

RUNNING STITCH

COUCHING

FISHBONE

BACK STITCH

PICTURE FRAME

*Easy to make in pretty colours, this picture frame is
an ideal introduction to the art of ribbon embroidery.*

Ribbons

- 1m (1¼yd) of 1.5mm (⅟₁₆in) wide lemon
- 50cm (20in) of 1.5mm (⅟₁₆in) wide dark green
- 2m (2¼yd) of 3mm (⅛in) wide mid blue
- 1m (1¼yd) of 3mm (⅛in) wide bright blue
- 1m (1¼yd) of 3mm (⅛in) wide royal blue

Other materials

- 14 count white Aida fabric 13cm by 11.5cm (5¼in by 4½in)
- Two pieces of mounting card each 11.5cm by 9.5cm (4½in by 3¾in)
- Piece of acetate 6.5cm by 9cm (2½in by 3½in)
- Latex fabric adhesive
- Clear general purpose adhesive

MAKING THE FRAME

1 With long tacking stitches mark out the finished size of the frame on the fabric following the measurements given.

2 Following diagram stitch the dots using French knots and the stem and leaves with five straight stitches.

3 Cut the centre from one piece of card as shown to form a frame.

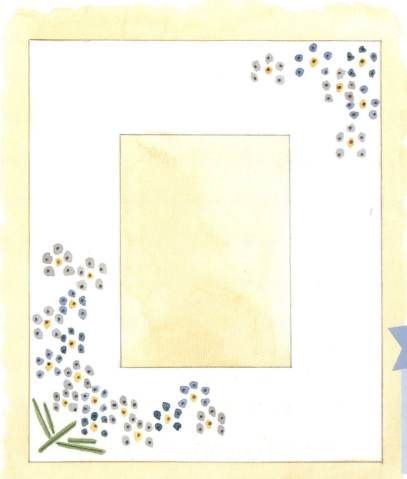

Blue (all shades) = French knot
Yellow = French knot
Green = Stem stitch

A couched trellis of narrow ribbon makes a perfect backdrop for creative floral embroidery. This Jacobean table runner features vibrant spring colours.

6 Stick the acetate to the wrong side of the frame with clear adhesive. When this is dry, stick the back mounting card to the frame on three sides with the clear adhesive, leaving the top edge open. Slide your photograph into this gap.

4 Stretch the fabric, right side facing outwards, over the card frame and stick at the back with fabric adhesive, mitring the corners for a neat, flat finish.

5 Cut out the centre of the fabric as shown, clip the corners, fold allowance to back of frame and stick in place.

7 To make a stand cut a triangle from the remaining card. Score a line 2cm (¾in) down from the top edge, bend this back and glue it to the back of the frame.

EMBROIDERED CARD

A lasting memento of that very important day, this beautiful embroidered wedding card can be framed to display for years to come.

MATERIALS

Ribbons

- six lengths of 23mm (⅞in) wide satin and taffeta in cream and white
- 30cm (12in) of 15mm (⅝in) wide cream satin
- 1m (1¼yd) of 1.5mm (¹⁄₁₆in) wide soft green satin
- 1m (1¼yd) of 1.5mm (¹⁄₁₆in) wide cream satin
- 1m (1¼yd) of 1.5mm (¹⁄₁₆in) wide white satin

Other materials

- Piece of white open-weave embroidery fabric 20cm by 25cm (8in by 10in)
- Piece of white card 20cm by 25cm (8in by 10in)
- Piece of white card 60cm by 25cm (24in by 8in)
- Sequins and beads

MAKING THE CARD

1 Make three stitched roses (see page 97) from the 23mm (⅞in) white ribbon and three from the cream.

2 Stitch roses to backing fabric. Fold a 5cm (2in) length of 15mm (⅝in) cream ribbon to make a flat rosebud, and stitch in place below the roses.

3 Embroider ferns using 1.5mm (¹⁄₁₆in) green ribbon, using an open fishbone stitch (see page 33). Sew loops of green ribbon among the roses to suggest foliage.

4 Using 1.5mm (¹⁄₁₆in) white ribbon, stitch French knots mixed with sequins, each applied with a small bead, to suggest gypsophila.

5 Using 1.5mm (¹⁄₁₆in) cream ribbon, stitch stephanotis on the right and left sides of the rosebud. For the flower heads on the left, make one short and three long stitches into the same hole. For those on the right, make five short stitches into the same hole.

6 Using the 15mm (¹⁄₁₆in) white ribbon, embroider lilies of the valley just below the roses with a cluster of French knots.

7 Finish with trailing ribbons, folded and attached with tiny stitches along edges.

8 Pin fabric out face down, lay the 20cm by 25cm (8in by 10in) card on top, fold edges.

9 Score and fold large card into three as shown on page 110.

10 On top section only, cut out a window in the front flap 12.5cm by 18cm (5in by 7in).

11 Glue embroidery behind window, then glue first two folds of card together to finish.

CHRISTMAS TABLE LINEN

Make your Christmas table extra special with this delightful tablecloth and matching napkins. Open Cretan stitch is used for Christmas garlands and wreaths.

THE EMBROIDERY

1 Draw up the motifs to size and transfer them onto the fabric corners using dressmaker's carbon paper. Note that the inner broken line is the stitch intersection point.

2 Using a tapestry needle, stitch the motif in dark green ribbon using Cretan stitch.

3 Secure loose ends by stitching them flat.

4 To finish, tie the tartan ribbon into bows (see page 82)

MATERIALS

Ribbon

For each napkin motif:
- 1m (1¼yd) of 1.5mm (1/16in) wide dark green doubleface satin
- 20cm (12in) of 15mm (⅝in) wide tartan

For each tablecloth corner motif:
- 1.25m (1½yd) of 1.5mm (1/16in) wide dark green doubleface satin
- 35cm (21in) of 15mm (⅝in) wide tartan

For tablecloth centre motif
- 4m (4½yd) of 1.5mm (1/16in) wide dark green doubleface satin
- 35cm (21in) of 39mm (1½in) wide tartan

Other materials
- Tablecloth and napkins in a moderately loose weave

MAKE-UP BAG

Worked in pastel shades this versatile basket of garden flowers could also decorate a dress pocket, picture, or dressing table accessories.

THE EMBROIDERY

1 Mark out the pieces on the fabric following the cutting diagram. Do not cut the fabric at this stage. Copy the design opposite onto tracing paper and, using dressmaker's carbon paper, transfer to the right side of the fabric.

2 Start by embroidering the basket, stitching ten vertical threads of ribbon as shown.

3 Work across with five horizontal threads weaving under one and over one, and the opposite on the way back. Couch a piece of the same ribbon along the top and base of the basket.

4 Follow the diagram and the stitch key to work the flower embroidery.

MAKING THE PURSE

1 When the embroidery is complete, cut out the fabric, lining and wadding using your traced outline as a pattern.

2 With right sides facing outwards sandwich the wadding between main fabric and lining and tack together around the edge.

MATERIALS

Ribbons – all 3mm (⅛in) doubleface satin
- 2m (2¼yd) light blue
- 2.50m (2¾yd) lilac
- 2m (2¼yd) pale yellow
- 1m (1¼yd) pastel green
- 50cm (20in) pale mauve
- 50cm (20in) coral
- 50cm (20in) white

Other materials
- Main fabric 25cm by 30cm (10in by 12in)
- Lining fabric 25cm by 30cm (10in by 12in)
- Wadding 25cm by 30cm (10in by 12in)
- Bias binding 90cm (35in)
- Zip 25cm (10in)
- Pale green embroidery thread 1m (1¼yd)
- Matching sewing thread
- Dressmaker's carbon paper

Fold

KEY TO STITCHES

1 French knot, light blue
2 French knot, lilac
3 French knot, white
4 Chain stitch, pastel green
5 Embroidery thread.
6 Pale yellow, couched with matching thread
7 Stem stitch, pale yellow
8 Five straight stitches, lilac
9 Five straight stitches, pale mauve
10 Coral stitch, pale pink
11 Stem stitch, pale green

3 Sew bias binding onto the top edge of each gusset piece. With wrong sides together, and matching notches and stars, join gusset pieces to sides of main pieces and machine.

4 Open up zip and machine each edge to inside of curved edges on both sides, tucking raw edges at top of zip into seam.

5 Bind the raw ends at other end of zip with bias binding or a small piece of left-over fabric.

6 Trim any excess wadding from the seam allowance, then bind the seams in one piece, machining the bias in place, then handsewing the free edge along the stitched line.

41

SAMPLER PANEL

Show off your ribbon embroidery skills on a traditional sampler. It would make a charming picture to hang on the wall appropriately finished with a picture bow (see page 87).

Chart A

MATERIALS

Ribbons – All doubleface satin (DFS) unless specified as singleface satin (SFS).

- 8m (8¾yd) of 1.5mm (¹⁄₁₆in) dark green
- 4m (4½yd) of 3mm (⅛in) antique blue
- 3m (3¼yd) of 3mm (⅛in) rose
- 2m (2¼yd) of 3mm (⅛in) sand
- 50cm (20in) of 23mm (⅞in) SFS red
- 1m (1¼yd) of 3mm (⅛in) dark purple
- 1m (1¼yd) of 3mm (⅛in) wine
- 1m (1¼yd) of 3mm (⅛in) navy
- 1m (1¼yd) of 9mm (⅜in) SFS maroon
- 25cm (10in) of 3mm (⅛in) bright blue
- 50cm (20in) of 3mm (⅛in) mid brown
- 50cm (20in) of 3mm (⅛in) white
- 50cm (20in) of 1.5 or 3mm (¹⁄₁₆ or ⅛in) black

Other materials

- 14 count white Aida fabric 26cm by 33cm (10½ in by 13in)
- Hardboard (or very strong , thick card) 22cm by 30cm (8¾in by 12in)
- Mid brown sewing thread
- Buttonhole thread
- Frame 22cm by 30cm (8¾in by 12in)

The sampler measures 21cm by 29.5cm (8¼in by 11¾in) and uses the following stitches and colours:

Border Double feather stitch – dark green. French knot – antique blue and rose.
Flower Basket Ribbon weaving – sand. Flowers, full and half – red.
Friezes Outlines in herringbone stitch – dark purple, wine, rose, navy. Leaves in lazy daisy stitch – dark green. Rosebud – maroon. Roseleaf in fishbone stitch – dark green. Bellflower – bright blue.
Tree Leaves in fishbone stitch – dark green. Trunk in couching – mid brown ribbon and matching sewing thread.
House Roof and door in running stitch and back stitch – antique blue navy. Flower stalks in fly stitch – dark green.
Sheep French knots – black, white.

THE EMBROIDERY

1 Mark the centre of the fabric by folding it in half vertically and then horizontally, pressing and then opening out. Work the central panel first from Chart A.

Chart D

Chart B

Chart C

2 Work the basket and handle from Chart B, starting with the handle. For the main part of the basket, work the short vertical stitches first. Leave the top and bottom horizontals unwoven and finish them with couching stitches.

3 Work the lower panel from Chart C and the borders from Chart D.

FINISHING AND MOUNTING

Place the backing card on the wrong side of the embroidery aligned to the margins. Fold the long edges of the fabric over the card and, working from the middle outwards, using buttonhole thread, lace back and forth, pulling tight. Repeat lacing on the short edges. The sampler can now be placed in the frame of your choice like a picture.

EMBROIDERED CUSHION

This enchanting posy of ribbon flowers makes a perfect keepsake. The flower motif could equally well be used to decorate a pretty wedding or christening card.

MATERIALS

Ribbons
- 2m (2¼yd) of 1.5mm (¹⁄₁₆in) wide doublefaced satin in each of the following colours – soft green, rose, mauve, light pink, cream
- 20cm (8in) of 15mm (⅝in) mauve
- 40cm (16in) of 9mm (⅜in) ivory
- 40cm (16in) of 9mm (⅜in) light pink
- 40cm (16in) of 9mm (⅜in) rose

Other materials
- Pink moiré satin 30cm by 115cm (12in by 45in)
- 2m (2¼yd) cream lace
- Heart shaped cushion pad
- Stitch and Tear interfacing
- Needle with large eye
- Three press studs
- Sewing threads to match fabric and lace
- Stranded embroidery cotton in cream and soft green

PREPARING THE FABRIC

1 Make a paper pattern from the diagrams, cut out the front and the two back cushion pieces from the satin fabric.

2 Using dressmaker's carbon paper, transfer embroidery design to the right side of the front piece of satin.

3 Tack a layer of Stitch and Tear to the wrong side of the front satin piece behind the embroidery design.

THE EMBROIDERY

1 Work the ribbon and cotton embroidery for the small flowers and leaves following the stitch and colour keys supplied. Use three strands of thread for the cotton embroidery. Use 40cm (16in) lengths of ribbon leaving about 2cm (¾in) of ribbon at

Scale 1 square = 12mm (⅜in)

back of work. When complete, neatly sew ends of ribbon flat using sewing thread.

2 Make a bow using oddments of 1.5mm (¹⁄₁₆in) wide light pink and mauve ribbon. Stitch in place at the top of green stems.

THE FLOWERS

Make flowers as follows.

MAUVE BELLFLOWER (1)

1 Take approx 6cm (2½in) of the 15mm (⅝in) wide mauve ribbon and fold raw ends to the wrong side.

2 Fold in half, stitching folded raw ends together.

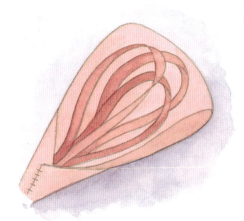

3 Now bring corners towards centre, turn in raw edges and stitch to secure.

4 Make loops with three lengths of 1.5mm (¹⁄₁₆in) wide rose. Tuck them inside bell and stitch in place.

LIGHT PINK GATHERED FLOWERS (2)

1 Take a 10cm (4in) length of 9mm (⅜in) wide ribbon and join along short ends to make a loop.

2 Run a line of gathering stitches around ribbon circle and pull up gathers to form a flower. Fasten off thread and stitch in place.

IVORY GATHERED FLOWER (1)

1 Make a gathered flower as above using ivory ribbon.

2 Make four small loops using 1.5mm (¹⁄₁₆in) mauve ribbon and tuck them into the centre of the flower. Stitch in place.

LOOP LEAVES (3)

For each set make three or four loops using 10cm (4in) strips of 1.5mm (¹⁄₁₆in) wide soft green ribbon. Stitch loops together.

ROSES

1 Make two stitched roses, one ivory and one rose, from 9mm (⅜in) ribbon as described on page 97.

as described on page 97.

KEY

1 Soft green ribbon couched with green stranded cotton.

2 Green stranded cotton straight stitch

3 Rose ribbon lazy daisy stitch

4 Mauve ribbon lazy daisy stitch

5 Light pink ribbon lazy daisy stitch

6 Cream ribbon lazy daisy stitch

7 Light pink ribbon French knots

All lazy daisy flowers have cream stranded cotton French knot centres.

MAKING UP THE CUSHION

1 Sew a line of running stitches along edge of lace and pull up to fit edge of front cushion. With the right side of the cushion facing and matching raw edges pin and tack the lace along stitching line.

2 Turn and machine 1cm (½in) to wrong side along the centre edge on both back pieces. With right side facing up, pin the two back pieces together, overlapping at the centre so they are the same size as the front piece.

3 With right sides together pin and machine around front and back pieces along stitching line. Remove all tacking threads and Stitch and Tear interfacing from the back of the embroidery.

4 Turn the cushion cover through the opening to the right side. Stitch the press studs in place on the back centre seam and insert cushion pad.

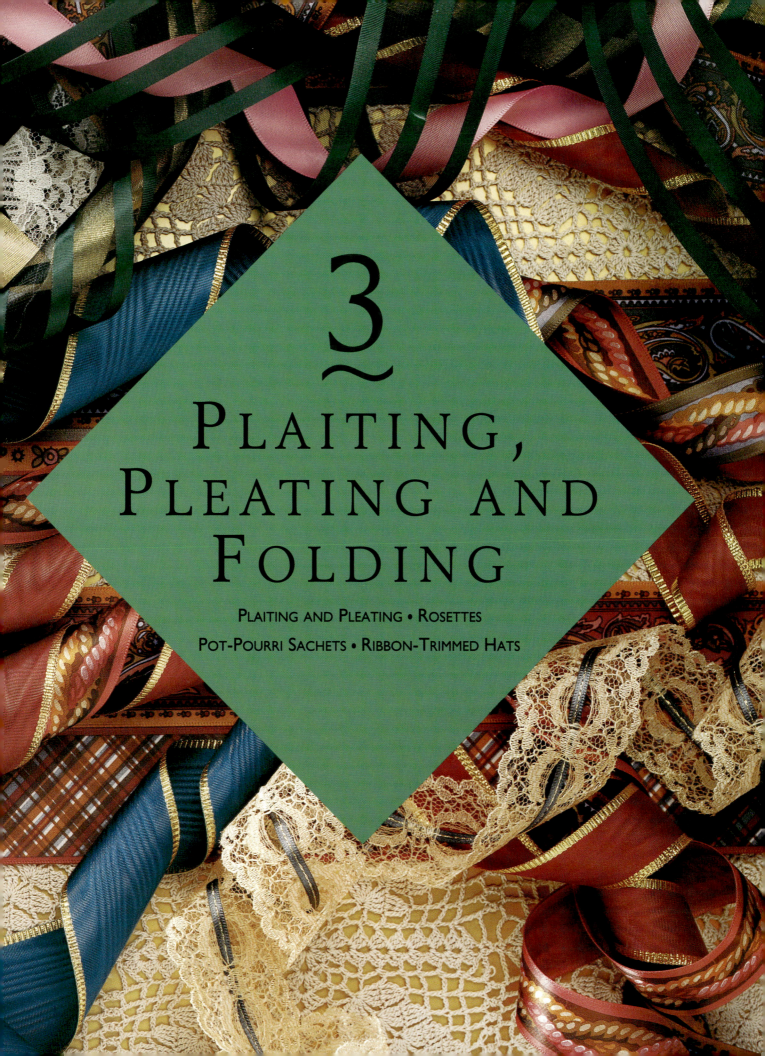

3
~
PLAITING,
PLEATING AND
FOLDING

PLAITING AND PLEATING • ROSETTES
POT-POURRI SACHETS • RIBBON-TRIMMED HATS

PLAITING AND PLEATING

*Conjure up a multitude of delightful rosettes and
trimmings by pleating, folding, plaiting and weaving
ribbons into three-dimensional forms.*

SIMPLE PLAIT

Plaited ribbon can be used to trim all kinds of objects. It is especially useful for appliqué work along curved edges for which straight-edged ribbon is not suitable.

1 Pin three strands of narrow ribbon together on a board.

2 Plait in the usual way, keeping right side of the ribbon facing throughout.

3 When you have completed the required length, stitch or knot at each end to secure.

FOLDED PLAIT

This method is particularly well suited to wide ribbon.

1 Pin three lengths of ribbon together on a board.

2 Plait, folding each outside strand towards the middle as you work. Stitch or knot at each end to secure when you have completed the required length.

FIVE-STRAND BRAID

This technique works best with narrow ribbon.

1 Pin five lengths of ribbon side-by-side on a board.

2 Working from one edge, bring the outside strand to the centre, taking it under the adjacent strand, over the next and so on as shown.

3 Repeat until your braid is the required length. Stitch at each end to secure.

LOOP BRAID

This type of braid can be left loose for a three-dimensional effect or be pressed flat.

1 Form a loop in one end of a ribbon (A). Form another loop (B) and pass through first loop.

SIMPLE PLEAT

You can create a variety of effects from pleated ribbon for use in appliqué work or as a trim. To calculate the amount of ribbon you need, treble the length of your intended finished pleat.

1 Fold and press the ribbon as shown.
2 Secure by topstitching either along one edge or down the centre according to the effect desired.

BOX PLEAT

Box pleated wide ribbon provides an attractive furnishing trim. Ribbon amounts are as for simple pleats.

1 Fold the ribbon as shown and press.

2 Take the long end of ribbon B, fold it to form a new loop and insert through the first loop.
3 Take the long end of ribbon B, fold to form a new loop and insert through the new loop in ribbon A.

3 Conceal the stitching with a length of appliquéd ribbon or ribbon plait.

2 Secure by topstitching along one edge or along the centre.
3 Conceal the topstitching as for simple pleats.

4 Continue until the required length is completed. Pin or stitch at each end to secure.

RIBBON BUTTON

This simple folded button provides a neat finish to rosettes and can also be used as a trim on its own.

1 Fold a length of ribbon in half as shown.

2 Fold left end under right (seen here on wrong side).

3 Turn to right side and continue to fold ribbon as shown.

4 Continue working in this way until button is completed.

5 Tuck loose ends under and stitch to secure.

GATHERING

Ribbon can be gathered in various ways to produce a number of different effects. The techniques depend largely on the type of ribbon used.

WOVEN-EDGE – SIMPLE GATHERING

1 Gather the woven-edge ribbon by machining a row of long loosely tensioned stitches along one edge or down the centre of the ribbon.

2 Pull the lower thread from one end to gather, easing the ribbon along its length as you work.

WOVEN-EDGE – SHELL GATHERING

A variation on simple gathering, this effect is produced by hand-stitching a zig-zag line down the length of the ribbon and gathering as above.

WIRE-EDGE

1 Gather wire-edge ribbon by freeing both ends of the wire from one edge of the ribbon. Secure one end by folding it over.
2 Pull the free end, easing the ribbon along its length to gather.
3 Trim excess wire and secure.

ROSETTES

Rosettes add a designer touch to home furnishings and clothing. Woven edge satin ribbon has been used on all the rosettes in this section.

RIBBON LILY

This 10.5cm (4½in) diameter rosette has 24 lily petals.

MATERIALS

- 2.10m (2½yd) of 39mm (1½in) wide ribbon

1 Form 24 petals as shown. After folding each petal, stitch at base to adjacent petal to hold in place.

2 When you have made 24 points, trim excess ribbon, overlap raw edges and stitch together, hiding seam inside last point.

3 Finish by concealing centre with a covered button, beads or ribbon rose in matching or toning colours.

RIBBON DAISY

1 Make a ribbon lily as described.

2 Before finishing, turn in alternate points and stitch to secure at centre.

FLAT RIBBON LILY

This can be made as an individual rosette sewn onto buckram or it may be sewn directly onto an item of clothing or home furnishing. For individual rosettes, in addition to the materials described for the ribbon lily above, you will need a circle of buckram or other fabric the diameter of the finished rosette.

1 Make a ribbon lily as described.

53

2 Pin each point to the buckram or fabric, ensuring they are facing in the same direction and are evenly distributed around its circumference. Stitch each point in place. Then stitch centre and add chosen finish.

ADDING LOOPS

If you are making an individual rosette, you may wish to stitch loops of contrasting or toning ribbon between each petal point. You will need an extra 2m (2¼yd) of 15mm (⅝in) ribbon.

1 Cut twenty-four 8cm (3¼in) lengths of ribbon. Fold each length in half and press.

2 Insert each loop between petal points, stitching to secure at base and point as shown.

FAN ROSETTE

This 18cm (7in) diameter semi-circular rosette is made from satin ribbon and uses four colours.

MATERIALS

- 1m (1¼yd) of 39mm (1½in) ribbon (colour A – outer pleat)
- 1.40m (1½yd) of 23mm (⅞in) ribbon (colour B – inner pleat)
- 1.40m (1½yd) of 23mm (⅞in) ribbon (colour C – outer row of points)
- 1m (1¼yd) of 23mm (⅞in) ribbon (colour D – inner row of points)
- 17cm (6¾in) diameter semi-circle of buckram.

1 Pleat colour A ribbon (see Simple pleating, page 51) and stitch through all layers around circumference of buckram, approximately 2cm (¾in) in from edge.

2 Secure back fold of each pleat through centre of width to buckram.

3 Pleat 70cm (28in) of colour B ribbon and stitch at base to buckram through all layers so that top of pleat overlaps the first row by approximately 1cm (½in).

4 Cut twelve 9cm (3¾in) lengths of colour C ribbon and eleven 9cm (3¾in) lengths of colour D ribbon. Fold each point as shown. Stitch to secure and press.

5 Stitch five colour C points (selvage side down) to buckram equally spaced under the second row of pleats so that the base of each point roughly aligns with the base of the pleat. Stitch a further four points of colour C between each point of previous row at same height.

6 Stitch five colour D points at equal intervals approximately 6mm (¼in) below previous row.

7 Stitch a further four colour D points between each one of previous row at same height.

FLORETTE ROSETTE

A rosette of this type can be made from woven edge (as here) or wire-edge ribbon. It would make a truly charming hair or hat decoration.

PETAL ROSETTE

This attractive spiral rosette can be finished with the centre of your choice. It is shown here with a florette centre and with a centre medallion.

PETAL ROSETTE WITH FLORETTE

8 Stitch one colour C point at centre 1cm (½in) lower than previous row, followed by two further colour C points on either side at same height.

MATERIALS

- 1.90m (2⅛yd) of 23mm (⅞in) gold edge ribbon
- 13cm (5¼in) diameter circle of buckram

1 Cut fourteen 13cm (5¼in) lengths of ribbon.
2 To make florettes, stitch raw ends of each ribbon length together and gather one selvage edge tightly.

MATERIALS

- 2.70m (3yd) of 23mm (⅞in) ribbon (colour A – petals)
- 25cm (10in) of 23mm (⅞in) wire-edge ribbon (colour B – outer florette)
- 18cm (7½in) of 23mm (⅞in) wire-edge (colour C – inner florette)

9 To make centre bow, cut 30cm (12in) of ribbon B and fold at centre as shown. Cut two 20cm (8in) lengths of ribbon B, fold each in half, stitch to tail fold and stitch the resulting bow to centre of rosette.

3 Stitch nine florettes evenly around circle of buckram, about 1cm (½in) in from edge. Stitch four florettes to form an inner circle and the last florette in the centre.

1 Cut twenty 12cm (5in) lengths of colour A ribbon.

10 Take the two remaining points of ribbon D. Tuck raw ends of one point inside the other and stitch over centre of bow.

2 Fold each length to form petals as shown and secure with a stitch or with bonding web (at base only).

3 Pin each petal to the buckram to form a spiral as shown. Stitch through buckram at centre and edge to secure.

3 Pin each petal to the buckram to form a spiral as shown. Stitch through buckram at centre and edge to secure.

4 Tightly gather one edge (see page 52) of ribbon B to create circle. Stitch raw ends together and stitch to centre of rosette.

5 Repeat above using ribbon C.

6 Make a stitched rose (see page 97) and stitch to centre of florette.

1 Cover buckram with fabric to make centre medallion. Turn to wrong side and stitch close to edge. Trim excess fabric.

2 Make 14 petal points from the 23mm ribbon.

CATHERINE WHEEL ROSETTE

This simple 8cm (3½in) diameter rosette can be made with or without tails.

PETAL ROSETTE WITH CENTRE MEDALLION

A rosette of this design was used to trim the ends of the Barrel Cushion on page 22.

3 Place in a spiral on the wrong side of the medallion as shown. Stitch or bond to secure at centre.

MATERIALS

- 1m (1¼yd) of 23mm (⅞in) ribbon
- 4cm (1½in) diameter circle of buckram
- A button covered with fabric or ribbon

1 Cut fourteen 5cm (2in) lengths of ribbon. Fold these in half and press.

4 Cut the 3mm ribbon into three equal lengths and make a simple plait (see page 50). Press and stitch around edge of medallion, folding raw edges of plait to wrong side. Stitch to secure and trim excess.

2 Catch corners together and pin ribbon pieces on buckram as shown. Stitch to buckram at centre to secure. Stitch button to centre.

3 Stitch equal lengths of spare ribbon to back of buckram to form tail if required.

MATERIALS

- 1.7m (66in) of 23mm (⅞in) ribbon
- 1m (39in) of 3mm (⅛in) ribbon
- 7cm (2¾in) diameter circle of matching fabric or wide ribbon
- 6cm (2½in) diameter circle of buckram

POT POURRI SACHETS

These pot-pourri sachets decorated with plaited, pleated and woven ribbon are a delightful way of bringing garden scents into the home.

ROUND SACHET

Ribbons (all singleface satin)
- 4m (4½yd) of 3mm (⅛in) wide in light colour
- 4m (4½yd) of 3mm (⅛in) wide in dark colour

Other materials
- One circle matching fabric 15cm (6in) diameter
- Two 15cm (6in) semi-circles of fabric plus 1cm (½in) seam allowance along straight edges
- Approximately 14cm (5½in) length of narrow Velcro
- 12cm (4¾in) square of iron-on interfacing
- Sewing thread

1 Cut twenty 12cm (5in) lengths of both the dark and light ribbon and prepare a zig-zag weave (see page 18) 10cm (4in) square.

2 Cut a 10cm (4in) diameter circle from the weave and machine with zig-zag stitches to centre of fabric.

3 Cut remaining light ribbon into three equal lengths and plait together. Do the same with the dark ribbon.

4 Cover raw edges of weaving with the light plait, and stitch in place.

5 Turn in a single hem along straight edges of fabric semi-circles and machine Velcro in place to close.

6 With right sides together machine around edges. Turn through to right side, handstitch dark plait around edge and fill with pot pourri.

SQUARE SACHET

Ribbons (all singleface satin)
- 40cm (16in) of 23mm (⅞in) dark green
- 1.80m (2yd) of 3mm (⅛in) dark green
- 30cm (12in) of 7mm (¼in) dark green

Other materials
- One piece fabric 17cm (7in) square
- Two pieces fabric 17cm by 9.5cm (7in by 3¾in)
- Short length of narrow Velcro

1 Fold one square of fabric across the diagonal and press to form guideline. Open out.

2 Make small pleats in 23mm (⅞in) ribbon until it is the same length as the diagonal line and machine in place along the centre.

3 Cut 3mm (⅛in) ribbon into three equal lengths and plait together.

4 Stitch three rows of plait: one in centre of pleated ribbon to cover stitching, and one across each corner, 5cm (2in) away from the central plait.

5 Make two small bows from 7mm (¼in) ribbon and stitch onto plaiting.

6 Turn in 1cm (½in) hems on two long edges of the back pieces, stitch in Velcro and finish as for round sachet, omitting plait trim.

RIBBON-TRIMMED HATS

Embellish a plain felt, straw or velvet hat with ribbon roses and rosettes to create your own unique look.

FELT HAT WITH LILY ROSETTE

The lily rosette with a coordinating outer circle of ribbon loops and a central cover button makes a dramatic hat trim (see page 53 for instructions for making the rosette). A band of ribbon in coordinating colors completes the trim.

WEDDING HAT

A very soft feminine look can be achieved with a dainty band of sheer ribbon entwined around a ribbon or cord hat band. This straw hat is perfect for a summer wedding or garden party.

FELT HAT WITH CATHERINE WHEEL ROSETTE

This delicate rosette and matching hat band in a rich printed satin ribbon discreetly complement the rich red of the hat. See page 56 for instructions for making the rosette.

VELVET HAT WITH SEMI-CIRCULAR ROSETTE

A thirties-style cockade finished with a central rose looks perfect on a cloche or similar period hat. A tail of ribbon at the top or bottom can add a touch of whimsy. Instructions for making the rosette are given right.

SEMI-CIRCULAR ROSETTE

This 15cm (6in) diameter rosette makes an original finish and can be seen on the hat above.

MATERIALS

- 1.40m (1½yd) of 15mm (⅝in) ribbon (colour A – first row)
- 1.10m (1¼yd) of 15mm (⅝in) ribbon (colour B – second row)
- 60cm (24in) of 15mm (⅝in) ribbon (colour C – third row)
- 11cm (4½in) diameter semi-circular piece of buckram

1 Cut ribbon into 8.5cm (3½in) lengths as follows: 10 colour A; 9 colour B; 6 colour C.

2 Fold ribbon A lengths in half and stitch equally spaced around curved edge of buckram as shown.

3 Form each length of ribbon B into petal points as shown and stitch to buckram under previous row. Each petal point should slightly overlap its neighbour.

4 Complete third row using six ribbon C points as second row.

5 Finish with a stitched rose in the remaining ribbon B (see page 97). Tails can be added if desired.

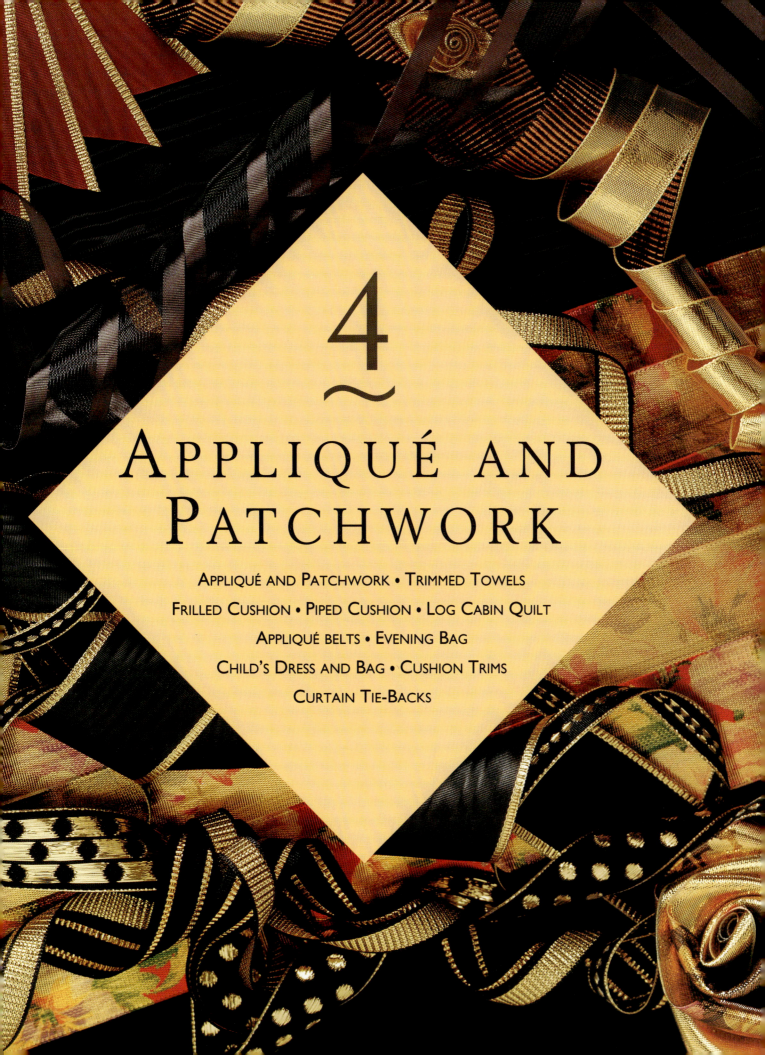

4

APPLIQUÉ AND PATCHWORK

APPLIQUÉ AND PATCHWORK • TRIMMED TOWELS

FRILLED CUSHION • PIPED CUSHION • LOG CABIN QUILT

APPLIQUÉ BELTS • EVENING BAG

CHILD'S DRESS AND BAG • CUSHION TRIMS

CURTAIN TIE-BACKS

APPLIQUÉ AND PATCHWORK

Woven-edge ribbons are simple to use for appliqué and patchwork. Because there are no raw edges they can easily be applied either by hand or machine sewing.

HELPFUL HINTS

- When machining, always work in the same direction on both edges to prevent puckering.
- Before you trim a garment with ribbon make sure it is colour fast and shrink resistant.
- Plan the design on paper to calculate quantities and widths. Remember to allow for seams and neatening ends.
- Ribbon is best applied to flat pieces of fabric before the garment is made up, but if trimming a ready made article, open up the seams a little to allow ribbon joins to be hidden inside the garment.
- Mark the design lines with dressmaker's chalk. Lay ribbon along the lines and position with a fabric glue stick or tacking stitches.
- When machining velvet, use a zipper foot to avoid crushing the pile.
- Use polyester thread, and if the ribbon puckers, try a larger stitch or loosen the top tension.
- If you prefer to handsew, use a tiny hem stitch.
- If you have a twin needle attachment adjust it to be slightly narrower than your ribbon so that you can stitch down both edges at the same time.
- If you have a large number of ribbons to sew next to one another, fix them onto lightweight iron-on interfacing before sewing.

IDEAS FOR RIBBON PATCHWORK

You can bring new dimensions to the time-honoured craft of patchwork using ribbon appliqué designs inspired by traditional patchwork quilts. Try any of the following designs, scaling the squares up or down by increasing or decreasing the rows of ribbons.

MISSOURI PUZZLE

This patchwork appliqué is worked directly onto fabric and the ribbon is woven at the intersections. The illustration shows 12 lengths of ribbon divided as follows (the widths of colours A, B, and C do not need to be the same): six green, four orange, and two yellow. Following the diagram, position and attach ribbons using fabric glue stick paying particular attention to woven intersections before stitching.

STRING QUILTED DIAMOND

Made from four small blocks joined to form a diamond effect on a large square. Each small square is worked on interfacing with ribbons stitched diagonally.

LOG CABIN PATCHWORK

In this type of patchwork light and dark ribbons are used to frame the small centre square.

COURTHOUSE STEPS

This is a log cabin variation constructed by stitching pairs of ribbons around the centre square. The pairs always match but a variety of light and dark shades of plain or printed ribbon can be alternated as the square is built up.

PINEAPPLE

The centre square of the pineapple is made from four horizontal ribbons. The next row consists of four ribbons placed diagonally across the corners. Raw edges are concealed by ribbons placed around the centre square. Continue the sequence with another set of diagonals and so on. The diagonals can be in a variety of shades and the straight ribbon in one colour or tones of a colour ranging from light to dark.

MITRED CORNERS

Mitring is a neat way of creating a right-angled corner with appliquéd ribbon.

1 Stitch ribbon to corner.
2 Lay ribbon end back along stitched edge.
3 Fold ribbon down to lie horizontally, making a diagonal fold at the corner; press lightly.

4 Stitch across diagonal fold line.
5 Continue stitching ribbon edge.

APPLYING RIBBON EDGINGS

Press the edge to be trimmed to right side of fabric. Tack the ribbon on the fold, covering the raw edge, then topstitch (wrong side first) along both edges of ribbon.

RIBBON CASINGS

Ribbon – at least 15 mm (⅝in) wide – makes an attractive casing for drawstrings or elastic in clothing or furnishing projects.

1 Press the top edge of the casing to the right side along seam line.
2 Trim to 6mm (¼in), and topstitch ribbon to right side of fabric, covering raw edge.
3 Fold in ribbon edges for the case opening. Run narrow ribbon through casing on a safety pin, and cut ends diagonally to prevent fraying. Ribbon casing can also be used as a way of neatening a raw edge.

TRIMMED TOWELS

Give plain towels a designer finish by applying a grosgrain ribbon trim, adding guipure lace for a special touch.

MATERIALS

- Ribbon to fit towel width plus turnings
- Lightweight iron-on interfacing
- Sewing thread
- Fabric glue stick

APPLYING THE RIBBON

1 Fuse lightweight iron-on interfacing to the wrong side of the ribbon, cutting the interfacing a fraction smaller than the width of the ribbon.

2 Position the ribbon on the towel and pin to secure. Turn the ends under and fix with fabric glue stick.

3 Machine the ribbon on with a small zig-zag stitch, working in the same direction on both edges, and stitch twice across the ends.

Basic bed and table linen can be luxuriously transformed with appliquéd ribbon. Choose plain or printed satins or jacquards to complement your existing colour scheme. And perhaps add a touch of lace or broderie anglaise.

FRILLED CUSHION

This cushion, with its appliquéd ribbons in deep, rich colours on a contrasting fabric, makes a bold statement.

Ribbons
- 2.70m (3yd) of 15mm (⅝in) wide patterned
- 1.30m (1½yd) of 23mm (⅞in) wide plain
- 2.70m (3yd) of 9mm (⅜in) wide plain

Other materials
- One cushion pad 35cm (13¾in) square
- 70cm (27½in) fabric 122cm (48in) wide
- 30cm (12in) zip

THE CUSHION PIECES

1 For the cushion front cut one 15in (38cm) square from the fabric. For the cushion back to include a zip, cut one piece 38cm by 32cm (15in by 12½in), and one piece 38cm by 10cm (15in by 4in).

2 With right sides together and using tacking stitches, join the back pieces with a 2cm (¾in) tacked seam. Machine stitch end sections outside zip length. Press seam open and pin, tack and then machine zip in final position.

WORKING THE APPLIQUÉ

1 On the cushion front, mark the centre point on each edge with a pin.

2 Fold each corner diagonally from pin to pin and press, then open fabric out again. The pressed creases will form guidelines for the ribbon.

3 Machine patterned ribbon along guidelines to form a diamond shape, then continue stitching ribbon in groups of five in the following order: patterned, plain 9mm (⅜in), plain 23mm (⅞in), plain 9mm (⅜in), patterned.

MAKING UP

1 From the remaining fabric, cut strips 10cm (4in) wide for the frill. With right sides together, join to make a 240cm (95½in) length.
2 Join ends to make a loop, then fold in half lengthways wrong sides together. Gather along raw edges through both thicknesses, and adjust to fit cushion front. With right sides together, pin and tack frill to front.
3 Open zip and then join back and front by pinning and then machining pieces with right sides together along seam line.

PIPED CUSHION

For a soft, rich effect, woven-edge ribbons in co-ordinating colours have been used for this cushion cover.

MATERIALS

Ribbons

- 4.50m (5yd) of 23mm (⅞in) wide patterned
- 2.30m (2½yd) of 23mm (⅞in) wide plain
- 4.50m (5yd) of 7mm (¼in) wide plain

Other materials

- One cushion pad 55cm (22in) square

- 1m (1¼yd) of 122cm (48in) wide glazed cotton
- 2.20m (2½yd) piping cord
- 45cm (18in) zip

2 Cover piping cord with bias strips and tack around edge of cushion front.

3 Machine piping to right side of cushion front along seam line.

4 With right sides facing, pin and machine front and back pieces together, using a machine piping foot if you have one. Turn through to right side and press.

THE CUSHION PIECES

1 From fabric cut one 58cm (23in) square for the cushion front. For the back, cut one piece 58cm by 50cm (23in by 19¾in); and one piece 58cm by 12cm (23in by 4¾in).

2 To make the cushion back, follow the instructions on page 65.

WORKING THE APPLIQUÉ

1 On the front square, mark 10cm (4in) in from each side horizontally and vertically with a pin.

2 Fold and lightly press across the marks to form guidelines for ribbons and sew them on with machine stitching in order as shown on the diagram.

MAKING UP

1 From remaining fabric, cut 3cm (1¼in) bias strips and join as shown to make a 220cm (88in) length.

LOG CABIN QUILT

In this log cabin quilt, plain satin ribbons in contrasting colours give a strong three-dimensional effect. For a larger quilt, simply increase the number of squares.

MATERIALS

Ribbons - all 23mm (⅞in) wide
- 1.20m (1½yd) shocking pink
- 12.50m (13½yd) aquamarine
- 12.50m (13½yd) jade
- 21.50m (23½yd) pink
- 24m (26yd) purple

Other materials
- 3.25m (4yd) cotton 112cm (44in) wide
- 2m (2¼yd) sew-in interfacing
- Sewing thread
- Press studs or Velcro
- Pencil and ruler

WORKING THE PATCHWORK

1 From interfacing cut 24 squares each 25cm (10in).

2 Draw diagonals from corner to corner on each square, using pencil and ruler.

3 Cutting ribbon to length as necessary, start by sewing on the central shocking pink ribbon square. Following diagrams, machine on ribbons, each time covering the edges of the previous ribbon.

4 Each square is worked in the same way. Complete the required number.

1

2

3

4

5

6

Scale I square = 5cm (2in)

JOINING THE SQUARES

1 Cut a piece of fabric 100cm by 150cm (40in by 60in) and tack all the patchwork squares in place.

2 Using the appropriate coloured ribbon (pink or purple) machine continuous strips to cover the edges of the squares and to form one large patchwork (the quilt top).

MAKING THE QUILT

1 From remaining fabric cut one piece 100cm by 145cm (40in by 57in) and one piece 9cm by 100cm (3½in by 40in).

2 Turn in 1cm (⅜in) along one short edge of each piece. Overlap edges by 1cm (⅜in) and fix Velcro or press studs to make case opening. If using press studs, make a narrow double seam. Velcro can be sewn over the raw edges.

3 With wrong sides together, tack front and back pieces together.

4 Cut two pieces of fabric 6cm by 150cm (2¼in by 60in) and use to bind sides of quilt.

5 Cut two pieces of fabric 6cm by 110cm (2¼in by 43¼in) and bind top and bottom edges.

APPLIQUÉ BELTS

Use appliqué techniques to create your own belts from ribbon in the colours, textures and prints that complement your wardrobe.

Simply cover a piece of substantial interfacing with bands of ribbon. First cut the interfacing to the desired finished size and shape. The length of a belt is the size of your waist plus turnings.

Use a fabric marker to work out positions for the ribbon and calculate the quantities accordingly. You can add further surface texture by incorporating embroidery stitches or applying narrow ribbon over wider bands using a straight or zig-zag stitch. Always take special care with the first ribbon as this will be your guide line for stitching all subsequent ribbons. Finish the edge of the belt with a ribbon plait or make a binding in the same fabric as your garment fabric.

Create your own belt designs to provide the perfect finishing touch to any outfit. Horizontal bands, diagonal stripes, toning colours or contrasting textures – the possibilities are endless.

Ribbon appliqué gives the opportunity for creating matching accessories. Here two black evening bags and a belt with appliquéd metallic ribbons would provide a sophisticated accent to a simple black outfit.

EVENING BAG

The magnificent ranges of Lurex and embroidered ribbons are perfect for decorating party accessories. This subtle Lurex print gives a plain bag a glamorous image.

THE BAG PIECES

Scale 1 square = 2cm(1¾in)

1 Make a paper pattern, following diagram, and cut out bag shape once in all fabrics. Tack taffeta piece to interfacing.

2 Machine the piece of metallic ribbon along the centre line, then machine lengths of 9mm (⅜in) grosgrain either side, butting up edges.

MATERIALS

Ribbons
- 60cm (24in) of 39mm (1½in) wide metallic floral
- 1.20m (1½yd) of 9mm (⅜in) wide gold grosgrain
- 10m (11yd) of 1.5mm (¹⁄₁₆in) wide gold grosgrain

Other materials
- One piece black taffeta 27cm by 82cm (10¾in by 32¼in)
- One piece heavy duty interfacing 27cm by 82cm (10¾in by 32¼in)
- One piece lining 27cm by 82cm (10¾in by 32¼in)
- Press stud

MAKING-UP THE BAG

1 Cut two side panels from taffeta and lining. On taffeta pieces, make darts, then sew to main piece to form a bag shape with flap.

2 Turn in all raw edges and hand-stitch in place.

3 Cut the 1.5mm (1/16in) grosgrain into three equal lengths. Plait together (see Simple plait, page 50) and handsew around flap edges and across top.

4 Cut remaining plaiting into two equal lengths and attach to either side of top to form shoulder strap.

5 Make up lining as main piece and handstitch into place.

6 To finish, sew press stud in place to fasten.

CHILD'S DRESS AND BAG

To make this pretty child's dress, look for a commercial paper pattern with a yoked design.

MATERIALS

Ribbons for dress – amounts according to measurements of hem, yoke and cuffs
- 39mm (1½in) printed
- 5mm (³⁄₁₆in) plain
- 15mm (⅝in) printed
- 3mm (⅛in) plain

Ribbons for shoulder bag
- 2.85m (3yd) of 23mm (⅞in) printed
- 90cm (3ft) of 5mm (³⁄₁₆in) plain
- 3.30m (3½yd) of 3mm (⅛in) plain

Other materials
- 45cm by 18cm (17¾in by 7in) heavy duty interfacing
- 45cm by 18cm (17¾in by 7in) lining
- One press stud
- Choice of pattern
- Materials as pattern
- Three ready-made roses

THE DRESS

1 Cut out pieces, following pattern instructions. Make up lower frill, shoulder frill, yoke front and back, and cuffs, but do not seam to rest of dress at this point.

2 Add ribbon to these pieces as follows:

3 To lower frill – one band each of 39mm (1½in) printed, 5mm (³⁄₁₆in) plain, 15mm (⅝in) printed.

4 To shoulder frill – one band each 15mm (⅝in) printed, 5mm (³⁄₁₆in) plain.

5 Centrally on yoke front and 5cm (2in) away each side – one band 5mm (³⁄₁₆in) plain, two bands 15mm (⅝in) printed.

6 Sew back yoke to match, omitting centre band.

7 On cuff – one band 15mm (⅝in) printed.

8 Make up dress as pattern instructions, and sew roses onto yoke.

9 Plait 3mm (⅛in) ribbon (see Simple plait, page 50) and stitch round collar edge. Sew roses on to yoke.

THE SHOULDER BAG

6 Turn to right side. Zig-zag stitch around raw edges of bag flap.

1 Make a paper pattern of the two bag pieces from the diagram, lay it on the interfacing and cut out a rectangle as shown.

2 Starting from one long side, sew ribbons vertically down the length of the interfacing in the following order: two rows wide printed, one row narrow plain. Continue in the same order.

3 Lay the pattern pieces on the ribbon-decorated interfacing and cut out the pieces. Cut the same pieces in lining. With wrong sides together, tack to interfacing.

4 Cut a 16cm (6¼in) piece of wide printed ribbon, fold it in half lengthways and sew over the raw edge at the top of the front pocket piece.

5 With right sides together, join front and back pieces with a narrow seam and finish with zig-zag stitching.

7 Plait 3mm (⅛in) plain ribbon and handstitch around petal edges. Use remainder to make shoulder strap, and sew to inside of front flap.

8 Sew on a press stud and ribbon roses.

Scale 1 square = 15mm (⅝in)

CUSHION TRIMS

These removable trims show a combination of appliqué and weaving, a novel way to embellish ready-made cushions. They are fastened at the back with Velcro.

Ribbons – all 7mm (¼in) wide except where indicated.

Pink cushion
- 16.80m (18¼yd) black A
- 18.50m (20¼yd) turquoise B
- 1.30m (1½yd) of 39mm (1½in) wide black

Purple cushion
- 17.70m (19¼yd) yellow A
- 17.70m (19¼yd) orange B
- 1.30m (1½yd) of 39mm (1½in) yellow

Turquoise cushion
- 11.80m (13yd) pink A
- 16.80m (18¼yd) mauve B
- 6.75m (7½yd) pale turquoise C
- 1.30m (1½yd) of 39mm (1½in) mauve

Blue cushion
- 6.75m (7½yd) pink A
- 6.75m (7½yd) sea green B
- 3.40m (3¾yd) yellow C
- 1.30m (1½yd) 39mm (1½in) wide sea green

Other materials (for each cushion)
- One 40cm (15¾in) square cushion pad
- 17cm (6¾in) square of craft-weight interfacing
- 17cm (6¾in) square of iron-on interfacing for weaving
- 12cm (4¾in) length Velcro

5 Cut 39mm (1½in) ribbon into four pieces, fold each one in half and enclose loose ribbon ends. Tack, then stitch to secure.

PINK CUSHION

1 Cut ribbon A and B into 84cm (33in) lengths.

2 Draw a 15cm (6in) square onto iron-on interfacing and zig-zag weave a square (see page 18), leaving 34.5cm (13½in) lengths of ribbon loose on all sides.

3 Place woven square in centre of heavy interfacing and machine around edge of weaving.

4 Carefully trim away excess interfacing close to machine stitches.

6 Cut Velcro in half and stitch to opposite ends of ribbon to fasten on underside of cushion.

TURQUOISE CUSHION

1 Cut ribbons A, B, and C into 84cm (33in) lengths.

2 Draw a 15cm (6in) square onto heavy interfacing and draw diagonals to find centre.

PURPLE CUSHION

1 Cut ribbons A and B into 84cm (33in) lengths.

2 Weave five warp B and five weft A at the centre of the heavy interfacing leaving 34.5cm (13½in) lengths loose as before.

3 Sew four B and then four A on each side of centre square in the order shown.

4 Continue from Step 4 of instructions for pink cushion.

3 Working from the centre out around the square, machine ribbons in the following order: one centre square of A, one of B each side of pink, two of C, four of B, three of A. Leave 34.5cm (13½in) lengths loose on all sides.

4 Continue from Step 4 of instructions for pink cushion.

BLUE CUSHION

1 Cut ribbons A, B and C into 84cm (33in) lengths.

2 Draw square as turquoise cushion. Working from outer edge inwards machine five rows of ribbon in the following order A, B, C, B, A.

3 Carefully trim interfacing from centre as well as outer edges.

4 Continue from Step 5 of instructions for pink cushion.

CURTAIN TIE-BACKS

*Evocative of hazy summer days, ribbons and roses give a
delightful feminine finish to piped tie-backs. Use ribbon
that matches your curtains to provide a subtle accent.*

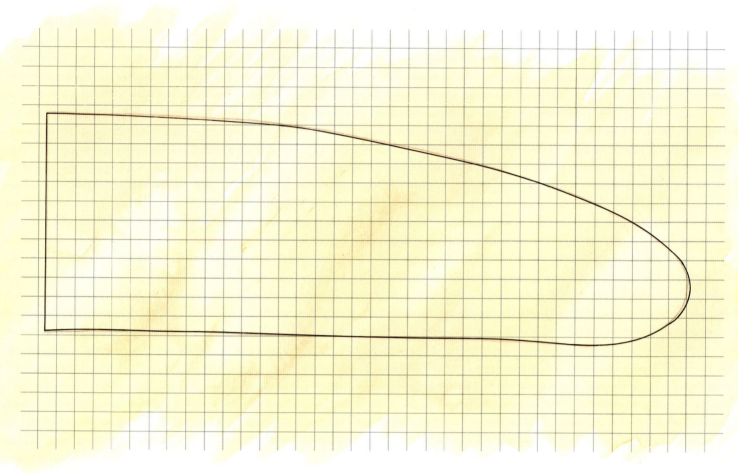

Scale I square = 1cm (½in)

MATERIALS

All quantities are for a pair.
- 2.50m (2¾yd) of 3mm (⅛in)
  doubleface satin ribbon
- 44 ribbon rosebuds
- 40cm by 80cm (16in by 32in) of fabric
- 40cm by 80cm (16in by 32in) of
  pelmet quality interfacing
- 40cm by 80cm (16in by 32in) of
  paper-backed adhesive
- 40cm by 80cm (16in by 32in) of lining
- 3m (3¼yd) No 3 piping cord
- Four by 2cm (¾in) rings
- Thread
- Fabric marking pen or pencil; ruler

The instructions are for two tie-
backs for a pair of curtains.

MAKING THE TIE-BACKS

1 Enlarge the grid diagram to make
a paper pattern and cut out two
pieces in fabric, two in interfacing
and two in lining.

2 Mark the centre of each fabric piece with a vertical line of tacking, then mark in a row of diagonal lines on the right side. They should be evenly spaced and 7.5cm (3in) apart. Mark in a second row in the opposite direction.

3 Machine the narrow ribbon in place with a small zig-zag stitch to cover the marked lines first in one direction, and then in the other to form a trellis.

4 Press paper-backed adhesive to one side of each of the interfacing pieces. When cool, peel off paper.

5 Press the adhesive side of the interfacing to wrong side of ribbon-trimmed fabric.

FINISHING

1 Cut and join enough bias strips 3.5cm (1⅜in) wide to fit around outer edges of tie-backs.

2 Cover piping cord with bias binding (see page 67) and apply to the trimmed and interfaced pieces with 13mm (½in) turnings.

3 Trim away the fabric on one side of the seam to layer it, press and tack towards the interfacing, bringing the piping to the edge.

4 Herringbone stitch the seam to the interfacing. Stitch roses at intersections of ribbon.

5 Trim off 6mm (¼in) all round on lining pieces. Turn under 6mm (¼in) all round, pin and hem to back of tie-backs. To finish, sew the rings 2cm (¾in) from the ends.

5
~

Bow-Making

Bow-Making Techniques • Picture Bow

Gift Wraps • Christmas Tree Bows • Christmas Basket

Easter Basket

BOW-MAKING TECHNIQUES

Bows are quick to make, using any type of ribbon.
Multiloop and layered bows suit more formal projects,
while hand-tied bows look pretty in informal arrangements.

USING A NAIL BLOCK

You can speed up the bow making process and produce consistent-sized hand-tied bows with a simple homemade nail block. Simply drive two nails through a wooden block (almost any offcut is suitable). The length of the nails and the distance between them determines the size of the finished bow, but they can be anything from 100mm (4in) to 250mm (10in) long. Simply loop the ribbon once or twice around the nails, pull tight and secure by tying the tails at the centre.

1 Arrange ribbon into two loops, holding one in each hand.

3 Fold left loop over right and under, tying into a bow.

2 Fold the right over the left.

CLASSIC HAND-TIED BOW

Use these traditional bows for decorating craft projects, gift wrappings or as a clothing trim.

Brightly coloured craft ribbon bows create an eye-catching finish to this cellophane-wrapped gift basket.

BASIC LOOP BOW

CENTRE BOUND BOW

DOUBLE BOW

These simple bows can be used on their own or combined to make other types such as layered bows.

1 Cut ribbon to twice the width of the finished bow plus a 5cm (2in) seam allowance and a little extra to allow for gathering the bow at the centre. Overlap the raw ends to form a loop, and stitch to secure.

1 Cut a length of ribbon three times the desired width of the bow, plus a little extra to allow for gathering. Cut the edges diagonally to prevent fraying.

2 Loop the ribbon loosely around as shown above.

These showy bows look complicated, but in fact are very easy to make. They are made in exactly the same way as the basic loop bow.

1 Make two loops, one larger than the other. The ribbon for the second bow can be the same width as the first or narrower.

2 With the stitched edge at centre back, flatten the loop slightly, pinch it together in the middle and either stitch down securely or bind florist's wire around the centre. The wire method is better for stiff ribbon.

3 Use florist's wire or a narrow ribbon of a matching or contrasting texture or colour to bind the centre. Ease the ribbon end at the front to the back of the bow. You can finish off with a hand-tied bow or bind the ribbon around several times and secure at the back.

2 Lay the small loop on the large one and bind with florist's wire, then wrap a short piece of ribbon around the wire, and either sew or knot at the back.

These looped bows are deceptively easy to make, and are ideal for decorating gifts or as hair accessories.

3 A tail can be added if desired, by sewing or gluing on two further pieces of ribbon at the back. Fix them at a slight angle, as shown.

2 The next length of ribbon is cut shorter than the first. The exact measurement depends on the effect you want to create. Make the loop in the same way, and place it centrally on top of the first one. Stitch through both layers at centre back, and pull stitches gently to gather the bow slightly.

1 Cut a piece of card 4cm by 8cm (1½in by 3in) and make a small hole on left-hand side 1cm (½in) in from the edge. Thread a length of florist's wire through the hole and around the card twice to secure.

LAYERED BOW

This bow takes the double bow one stage further by using several different-sized loops joined together. The ribbon for each layer should be the same width, and you can either make them all in the same colour or vary them.

1 To make the base, or back of the bow, cut ribbon to desired length plus 2.5cm (1in) seam allowance. Overlap ends to form a loop, stitch, and flatten out loop.

3 Continue in the same way, making each layer shorter, until you have as many as you want. Finally, wrap a short length of ribbon around the centre and stitch at back.

2 Working from left to right on top of the card make ribbon loops, securing each one with a turn of the wire. Leave a 10cm (4in) ribbon tail at each end.

3 Secure wire on underside of card by twisting it around itself, cutting off the end.

POMPON BOWS

A pompon bow is made from many loops of ribbon which are anchored tightly at the centre with florist's wire before being separated to form a fluffy bow. The average pompon bow requires 3.20m (3½yd) of ribbon.

1 Begin with a loop of ribbon about 15cm (6in) across (you can adjust the size for a larger or smaller bow).

2 Wrap the ribbon around 10 times.

3 Flatten the loops and cut off triangles at each end as shown.

4 Bring the ends together in the middle, matching the cut triangles.

5 Wrap centre with wire, and pull out loops, twisting them as you turn.

A basket wrapped in netting and trimmed with a sheer multiloop bow provides a touch of luxury to a simple gift.

MULTILOOP AND FLORIST'S BOWS

Wreaths and flowers often need ribbons arranged among them, with cones and other display materials to add colour and texture. Florist's loops and bows have a small base and full top. The method for making them is similar to that for pompon bows, but the loops are squeezed upwards and secured with wire to keep them upright.

1 Take a length of ribbon, about 1.80m (2yd), and squeeze it between your fingers approximately 5cm (2in) from one end.

2 Hold ribbon in one hand and make a loop in it with the other; pinch ribbon and hold securely.

3 Add another loop to the other side of bow and pinch as before, twisting ribbon as necessary to keep right side of ribbon to the outside of the bow.

4 Continue making loops, alternating from side to side and pinching each one firmly in the centre until at least four loops have been made on each side.

5 To secure, wrap wire around centre of bow and twist firmly. Pull loops into shape.

6 To turn this into a florist's bow, simply make a small loop in the centre with the last tail and wire to secure.

Impressive to look at but easy to make, our traditional florist style bow is suitable for almost every occasion. Use them for decorating a floral arrangement, tying up a wrapped package or gift basket or finishing off a wreath or garland, or decorating a room for a special occasion. The technique is versatile and any size or type of ribbon can be used. You can design your bow as you make it.

PICTURE BOW

Enhance a picture with a bow centred above the frame, or make a group arrangement in colours to match the frame or mount.

MATERIALS

- 2.80m (3yd) of 39mm (1½in) wide moiré taffeta ribbon
- 2.80m (3yd) of 56mm (2¼in) wide singleface satin ribbon
- Hemming web
- Florist's wire

1 Placing the 39mm (1½in) ribbon centrally on the wider one, bond the two pieces of ribbon to each other using hemming web.

2 Make two loops about 10cm (4in) wide, with a small overlap in the middle and bind in the middle with florist's wire.

3 Cover the wire with a piece of ribbon, securing it at the back with a couple of stitches.

4 Stitch bow tails of whatever length you require at the back of bow, and finish with a loop to attach to a picture hook.

GIFT WRAPS

Have fun choosing ribbon colours and prints to match the mood of the occasion. Soft and romantic, bright and amusing, or simply wild.

Multiloop bows (see page 86) are a popular choice for gift wraps. It is up to you to decide how many loops, the length of the tails and what style to have the centre. To determine how much ribbon each bow will need first decide how long each loop will be and multiply that amount by two, then multiply this figure by the number of loops that you want. Add the total length of the desired tail ends to that figure and round up by about 10cm (6in) to get the total amount needed for creating your style bow.

A patterned ribbon has been used to bind the parcel (below) and a multiloop bow in yellow and red provides the finish.

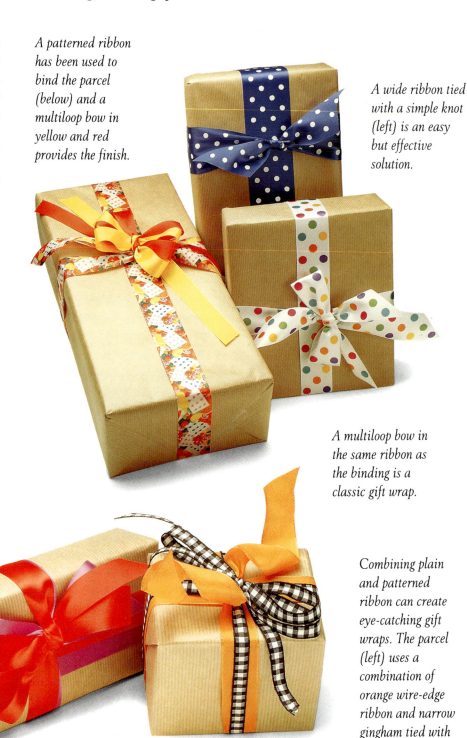

A wide ribbon tied with a simple knot (left) is an easy but effective solution.

A multiloop bow in the same ribbon as the binding is a classic gift wrap.

Red and pink ribbons have been worked together (right) and tied in a multiloop bow.

Combining plain and patterned ribbon can create eye-catching gift wraps. The parcel (left) uses a combination of orange wire-edge ribbon and narrow gingham tied with a multiloop bow.

Patterned ribbon for binding with a sheer multiloop bow (below) produces a delightfully soft effect.

The bold daisy pattern of this wide ribbon (left) needs no more elaborate finish than a centre knot. Long ribbon tails give a hint of luxury.

Three types of ribbon have been used for this luxurious parcel (above right). Wide patterned ribbon simply knotted has been used for the binding. The central multiloop bow is a combination of plain wide ribbon and several colours of narrow ribbon.

Two wire-edged ribbons are used here. A purple ribbon tied in a simple knot binds the parcel and a wide pink ribbon is used for a single bow at the centre with generous curled tails.

A multiloop bow in sheer striped ribbon topped with a stitched rose creates a soft, feminine gift wrap.

The bold effect here is created by the strong patterning of the ribbon which is tied in a loose multiloop bow.

CHRISTMAS TREE BOWS

All kinds of bows can be used to decorate a tree either on their own or together with other trimmings.

1 Wind ribbon around the nail block, keeping ends of even length. Take care not to injure yourself on the sharp points.

MATERIALS

For each bow you need 70cm (28in) of 39mm (1½in) wire-edge taffeta ribbon.

You can make all your bows in the same colour as shown here or use different colours. The bow used for this tree is a single bow made on a 12.5cm (5in) wide nail block.

2 Tie ends at back and round centre of bow.

3 Cut ribbon ends into fishtails

4 Attach to tree with florist's wire

A simple picture bow made up in Christmas ribbon is a great way to display your Christmas cards.

This cut edge tartan multi-loop bow has a centre wire, which makes shaping possible after the bow is formed. A perfect decoration for garlands and extra special gifts.

A wreath bound in tartan and finished with a double loop bow looks pretty on the tree. Alternatively make a pair to adorn each side of the fire place.

A handsome double loop bow in plaid or plain taffeta gives a festive touch to a Christmas table setting or the children's Christmas stockings.

CHRISTMAS BASKET

Decorate a simple basket by weaving ribbon through the side panels. Straight-sided shapes are easiest to work. Add a pretty bow for a finishing touch.

MATERIALS

Ribbons

- 68mm (2⅞in) wide cotton emerald, length of 60cm (24in) plus circumference of basket
- 60cm (24in) of 39mm (1½in) wide acetate red
- 60cm (24in) of 23mm (⅞in) wide wire-edge polyester dark green

Other materials

- Loosely woven cane basket
- Assorted grasses, dried flowers and fruit
- Binding wire
- All-purpose clear adhesive.

DECORATING THE BASKET

1 Weave the emerald ribbon carefully through the open lattice of the basket, overlapping the ends and joining them neatly with a spot of glue.

2 Make a large multiloop bow (see page 86) from the remaining emerald ribbon, secure with a long length of binding wire, cut ends of ribbon at an angle.

3 Make similar bows from the other two ribbons. Arrange the bows in your hand one on top of the other, and bind together with the long wire of the cotton bow.

4 Wire the multiloop bow to the inner rim at one end of the basket.

5 Arrange the grasses, flowers, and fruit in position and glue in place.

EASTER BASKET

What better way to present colourful Easter eggs than in this pretty basket you have decorated yourself with satin, lace and gingham bows.

MATERIALS

Ribbons
- 3m (3¼yd) of 23mm (⅞in) wide yellow singleface satin
- 3.80m (4¼yd) of 15mm (⅝in) wide lace and yellow cut-edge
- 2.40m (2¾yd) of 23mm (⅞in) wide gingham
- 80cm (32in) of 15mm (⅝in) wide lace cut-edge

Other materials
- Basket with handle
- Assorted dried grasses and small flowers

DECORATING THE BASKET

1 Make three bows from the 23mm (⅞in) gingham and a florist's or multiloop bow from 80cm (32in) of the 15mm (⅝in) wide lace cut-edge ribbon.

2 Bind handle with 1m (1¼yd) 23mm (⅞in) singleface satin ribbon, and glue in position at either end.

3 Bind 1m (1¼yd) lace cut-edge over the top of the satin ribbon and glue. Repeat binding around the rim of the basket.

4 Glue small pieces of dried grasses and small flowers along the ribbon edge, carefully hiding the stalks under the ribbon.

5 Attach two gingham bows at either end of handle, and one at the centre top of handle.

Layers of looped ribbons cascading down the handle of plain baskets and trimmed with bows or roses at the sides make perfect gift baskets or decorative containers for floral arrangements or for the dressing table.

6

ROSE-MAKING

ROSE-MAKING TECHNIQUES • FESTIVE TABLE-CENTRE

BRIDAL HEAD-DRESS • BRIDE'S BOUQUET • ROSE BALL

WEDDING TABLE-CENTRE • ROSE-TRIMMED PARCELS

ROSE-MAKING TECHNIQUES

Ribbon roses are incredibly versatile: they can decorate bridal wear, hats, shoes, accessories, and add finishing touches to many other projects.

RIBBON QUANTITIES

The width of the ribbon determines the amount you need for making one rose or rosebud. You can make a tiny stitched rose with 7mm (¼in) wide ribbon but anything less than 15mm (⅝in) is too fiddly for the stemmed variety. The chart shows how much ribbon you need for each rose according to width. To work two ribbons together, double the amount.

WIDTH OF RIBBON	LENGTH OF RIBBON	
	Stemmed & Stitched Roses	Rosebuds
5mm (³⁄₁₆in)	13cm (5in)	
7mm (¼in)	20cm (8in)	8cm (3in)
9mm (⅜in)	20cm (8in)	8cm (3in)
15mm (⅝in)	40cm (16in)	15cm (6in)
23mm (⅞in)	50cm (20in)	15cm (6in)
39mm (1½in)	80cm (32in)	40cm (16in)
56mm (2¼in)	1.25m (1½yd)	50cm (20in)

BASIC METHODS

For floral arrangements, corsages and parcel trims, the ribbon roses are made on stem wires, but for most fabric projects they are hand stitched. Both versions are basically made in the same way.

TENSION

The tighter you fold and twist the ribbon, the smaller the finished rose will become, so it will look larger, softer and more open if you work it loosely. By varying the tension of every rose you will create a spray of unique blooms – just as if they had been picked from the garden.

Wire edge ribbons made into bows and roses look great – whether you choose one rose or a cluster of 3 or more. Here, an ombré taffeta rose with lavish tails produces a stylish summer look.

STEMMED ROSE

This rose is made on a wire, so in addition to ribbon you will also need a length of stub wire, some florist's binding wire and stem binding tape. You can finish off with artificial rose leaves if you like.

1 Bend the end of the stub wire into a loop. Thread and fasten a piece of binding wire around to secure it.

2 Fold ribbon end over the loop and gather it around stem, tightly winding the binding wire around three times.

3 Pull end of ribbon up and then out sideways.

4 Roll the ribbon around four times to form a tight tube and secure with binding wire.

5 Make each petal by first diagonally folding the ribbon end away from you.

6 Turn bud onto centre of fold. The bud must always lie inside the rose and come below the edge of the fold. Continue turning bud onto fold until ribbon is straight again, making a cone shape around the bud. Let the binding wire twist itself around the base of the rose as you work, pulling it tight each time you make a petal. Continue making petals until the rose is of the desired size.

7 Bring end of ribbon down to base of rose. Grip it firmly in one hand and wind the binding wire tightly around the base of rose, to secure.

8 Lay the end of the stem binding tape directly under the rose head and press, stretching it slightly. Turn rose, pressing the tape over the wire to cover it, binding in an artificial leaf if required.

STITCHED ROSE

Whether the roses are made on stem wires or stitched, the process is basically the same. Your only requirement, apart from the ribbon, is a matching thread and a needle.

1 Roll ribbon into a tight tube, making four turns, and stitch bottom of tube to form bud of rose.

2 Now follow the method for the stemmed rose up to step 7 but stitch the base after each turn instead of binding with wire.

WIRE-EDGE RIBBON ROSE

Lengths of wire-edged taffeta make beautiful cabbage-type roses that give a very different effect from the folded versions.

1 Simply draw up one edge of the wire, fastening it at the other end to stop the whole length of wire coming through.

2 Turn in the raw end and gather the ribbon up tightly so that it coils around itself to form a flower shape.

3 Use the drawn up wire to bind the base of the rose, or stitch with needle and thread.

RIBBON ROSETTE

This method of making a rose works particularly well with paper and cut-edge ribbons. It principally involves folding and finally pulling through and twisting, and gives yet another look to our rose collection. Just follow the diagrams below.

FESTIVE TABLE-CENTRE

This stylish dinner party decoration shows how a clever choice of ribbon – floral printed metallics – can transform the look of a basic arrangement.

MATERIALS

Ribbons
- 4.20m (4¾yd) of 39mm (1½in) wide metallic
- 2m (2¼yd) of 9mm (⅜in) wide metallic

Other materials
- Gold candle and four cocktail sticks
- Seven artificial gold leaves
- Thirty gold baubles
- Six poppy seedheads sprayed gold
- Circle of card approx 14cm (5½in) diameter
- Black felt to cover card
- Small piece florist's foam about 6cm (2½in) diameter by 3cm (1¼in) high

5 Arrange the baubles in groups of six and twist the stems together.

6 Arrange roses, bows, baubles and other decorations around candle, completely covering foam.

MAKING THE TABLECENTRE

1 Make seven stemmed ribbon roses from 39mm (1½in) wide ribbon. The stems need only be about 5cm (2in) long.

2 Make four wired multiloop bows (see page 86) from 9mm (⅜in) wide ribbon.

3 Cover the card with black felt, and glue the florist's foam to the centre.

4 Tape the cocktail sticks to the bottom of the candle and position in centre of foam.

This stunning corsage can be worn on an evening dress, attached to a bag or belt, or worn in your hair. It's quickly made by wiring together two multiloop bows, a ribbon rose and a few gold baubles and leaves. You could adapt the idea, choosing your ribbons and baubles to match a favourite outfit.

99

BRIDAL HEADDRESS

This pretty circlet of ribbon roses with artificial flowers, pearl beads, ribbon loops and streamers is perfect for a bride or bridesmaids.

MATERIALS

Ribbons

- 2m (2¼yd) of 56mm (2¼in) wide doubleface satin ivory
- 1.5m (1¾yd) of 3mm (⅛in) wide pink
- 1.3m (1½yd) of 39mm (1½in) wide white sheer
- 2m (2¼yd) of 23mm (⅞in) wide taffeta pink
- 1.5m (1¾yd) pearl beading
- Wadding
- Florist's stub wire and stem wraps
- Thirteen small artificial flowers
- All-purpose glue

RIBBONS AND BOWS

1 Make four stemmed ribbon roses (see page 96) using the 23mm (⅞in) wide pink taffeta ribbon.

2 Make two multiloop bows with tails (see page 86), one from the 39mm (1½in) wide white ribbon and one from the 3mm (⅛in) wide pink ribbon.

MAKING THE HEAD-DRESS

1 Measure the bride's or bridesmaid's head and make a wire ring to fit using several florist's stub wires bound together with stem wraps.

2 Cover the wire ring with wadding and then wrap with the doubleface ivory satin ribbon, stitching the ends at the back. Carefully wind the beading and narrow pink ribbon evenly around the ring.

3 Make up two small sprays with the roses and small artificial flowers, covering the stems with stem wrap. Stitch and glue the sprays at the back of the head-dress leaving a 6cm (2½in) space.

4 Stitch and glue the sheer and narrow ribbon bows together in the centre of the space between the flower sprays.

5 Glue a small artificial flower into the centre of the bows and trim the tails to length.

BRIDE'S BOUQUET

Choose ribbons in a colour combination to suit the occasion, and to ring the changes, add dried, natural or artificial flowers or different ribbons.

MAKING THE BOUQUET

1 Mount the white sheer bows on florist's stub wires and use more florist's tape to bind each one to the stem of an ivory rose, about 3cm (1¼in) below the flower.

2 Mount the other bows on shorter lengths of florist's stub wire.

3 Group the roses and sheer bows into a posy in your hand, with some of the larger ones above or below others. Bind together with wire, keeping the binding in one place for a neat finish.

4 Add the smaller roses and flower sprays and bind into position, then bind in the large striped bows at the bottom.

5 To form the handle, cut the stems below the binding to approx 15cm (6in).

6 For a neat finish, bind the two ivory taffeta bows in place at the top of the handle under the bouquet.

7 Cover the handle with stem tape and then cover with the ivory taffeta.

ROSES AND BOWS

Make the following stemmed ribbon roses (see page 96). The stems need to be about 25cm (10in) long.

Nine large roses from the 56mm (2¼in) wide cream with gold wire-edge

Ten smaller roses from 23mm (⅞in) wide pink taffeta

Make the following multiloop bows (see page 86):

Five bows from 39mm (1½in) wide white sheer

Three larger bows from 39mm (1½in) wide white sheer with stripes

Two bows from the 23mm (⅞cm) wide ivory taffeta

MATERIALS

Ribbons

- 6.3m (7yd) of 56mm (2¼in) wide cream with gold wire-edge
- 5m (5½yd) of 23mm (⅞in) wide pink taffeta
- 5m (5½yd) of 39mm (1½in) wide white sheer
- 4.5m (5yd) of 39mm (1½in) wide white sheer with satin stripes
- 1m (1¼yd) of 23mm (⅞in) wide ivory taffeta

Other materials

- Ten small artificial flower sprays
- Florist's stub wire, binding wire and stem tape

This corsage is based on a single stemmed rose, embellished with bows.

101

ROSE BALL

A pretty accessory in pink satin ribbon for a bridesmaid to carry. Coordinate the ribbon colours of the dress and head-dress for a stunning effect.

MAKING THE BALL

1 Pierce the dry-foam ball through its centre with the stub wire, then bend each protruding end of the wire to form a small loop.

2 Cut each of the 3mm (⅛in) wide ribbons in half. Take one length of each shade and slip through one of the stub wire loops then knot ends to form a hanging loop.

3 Next thread the remaining three ribbons through the other stub wire loop on the ball to create a tail, securing them with a pearl-headed pin.

4 Make 72 stitched roses (see page 97) from the six different shades of 15mm (⅝in) ribbon.

5 Divide the ball into six sections and outline with cloves. Place remaining pearl-headed pins equally spaced along each line of cloves. Fill each section with 12 roses of one shade, attaching each one with a pin.

6 Cut the 23mm (⅞in) wide ribbon into four equal lengths and fold and wire each length into a centre-bound bow (see page 83). Insert two bows at each end of ball close to tail and close to hanging loop.

7 Make up six stitched roses from 7mm (¼in) ribbon and stitch each one to a contrasting coloured ribbon tail. Glue pearl beads to top bow to finish.

WEDDING TABLE CENTRE

This romantic arrangement of flowers and ribbons in bridal colours with matching candle is guaranteed to set the festive mood for a great occasion.

MATERIALS

Ribbons

- 5.4m (6yd) of 9mm (⅜in) wide green feather-edge
- 3.2m (3½yd) of 23mm (⅞in) wide white sheer
- 1.8m (2yd) of 39mm (1½in) wide pink satin
- 2m (2¼yd) of 23mm (⅞in) wide pink taffeta
- 4m (4½yd) of 23mm (⅞in) wide cream taffeta
- 3m (3¼yd) of 39mm (1½in) wide cream sheer

Other materials

- Eight small flower sprays
- One pink candle
- One candle holder or four cocktail sticks and clear adhesive tape
- Piece of dry florist's foam or styrofoam
- 20cm (8in) diameter cake board
- All-purpose glue

ROSES AND BOWS

1 Make the following stemmed ribbon roses:

Three from the 39mm (1½in) wide pink satin

Four from the 23mm (⅞in) wide pink taffeta

Eight from the 23mm (⅞in) wide cream taffeta

Five from the 39mm (1½in) wide cream sheer

2 Following the instructions on page 86, make nine multiloop bows from the 9mm (⅜in) wide green feather-edge and four from the 23mm (⅞in) white sheer

ASSEMBLING THE TABLECENTRE

1 Glue the dry foam or styrofoam to the centre of the cake board.

2 Position candle in holder or use clear adhesive tape to bind cocktail sticks to the base of the candle, position candle in the foam.

3 Arrange the roses and bows around the candle so that the foam is covered.

A single ribbon rose on a long stem makes a simple and elegant napkin ring (left). Choose a colour to link in with table decorations. A soft finish is achieved by trimming the satin ribbon with sheer bows and streamers.

ROSE-TRIMMED PARCELS

These prettily decorated parcels are easy to make once you have mastered the rose making techniques – a lovely way to make any gift extra special.

MATERIALS

Singleface satin ribbon
- 40cm (16in) of 3mm (⅛in) wide pale pink
- 40cm (16in) of 3mm (⅛in) wide pale blue
- 40cm (16in) of 3mm (⅛in) wide cream
- 50cm (20in) of 7mm (¼in) wide pale pink
- 90cm (1yd) of 15mm (⅝in) wide mid-pink
- 1.60m (1¾yd) of 23mm (⅞in) wide deep pink

Sheer stripe ribbon
- 70cm (27in) of 39mm (1½in) wide

Satin printed ribbon
- 23mm (⅞in) wide to wrap the length and width of parcel A
- 35mm (1½in) wide to wrap the length and width of parcel B

Other materials
- Fabric or wrapping paper for the two parcels
- About 30cm (12in) of pearl beading
- Six silk rose leaves
- Florist's wire and stem wrap
- Double-sided clear adhesive tape

WRAPPING

Wrap the parcels tightly in the fabric or paper. Circle the parcels along their lengths and widths with satin printed ribbon, sealing the ends neatly on top with adhesive tape.

PARCEL A

1 Make an assortment of ribbon roses and rosebuds on fine wire stems from three of the pink ribbons. Use the whole length of the 7mm (¼in) wide ribbon, a 25cm (10in) length of the 15mm (⅝in), and a 75cm (30in) length of the 23mm (⅞in) ribbon. Do not wrap the wires in stem wrap.

Stemmed roses can be the basis of many charming decorative treatments. You can make them more elaborate by adding leaves, loops and bows.

2 Using the three lengths of 3mm (⅛in) ribbons, wire a ribbon loop as shown in the illustration.

3 Wire the pearl beading into four individual loops. Assemble the roses, leaves and buds in your hand, slip the beading loops in at the back, and

bind together with one of the wire stems of a rose. Cover the combined stems with stem wrap.

4 Add the ribbon loop below and in front of the largest rose and stick the spray to the parcel.

PARCEL B

1 Make an assortment of five roses and two to three rosebuds on fine wire stems, using the remaining 65cm (26in) of 15mm (⅝in) wide

ribbon and the remaining 85cm (34in) of 23mm (⅞in) ribbon. Do not stem wrap the wire stems.

2 Fold and wire a double bow (see page 83) from sheer stripe ribbon, slanting the ends, and tape it to the top of the parcel.

3 Assemble the roses, leaves and buds in your hand and bind together with the wire stem of one of the roses, then cover combined stems with stem wrap.

4 Stick the spray to the centre of the sheer bow with double-sided tape.

These delightfully unusual parcels are trimmed with stemmed roses and rosebuds, with pearl beading and multiloop bows giving an extra touch of luxury.

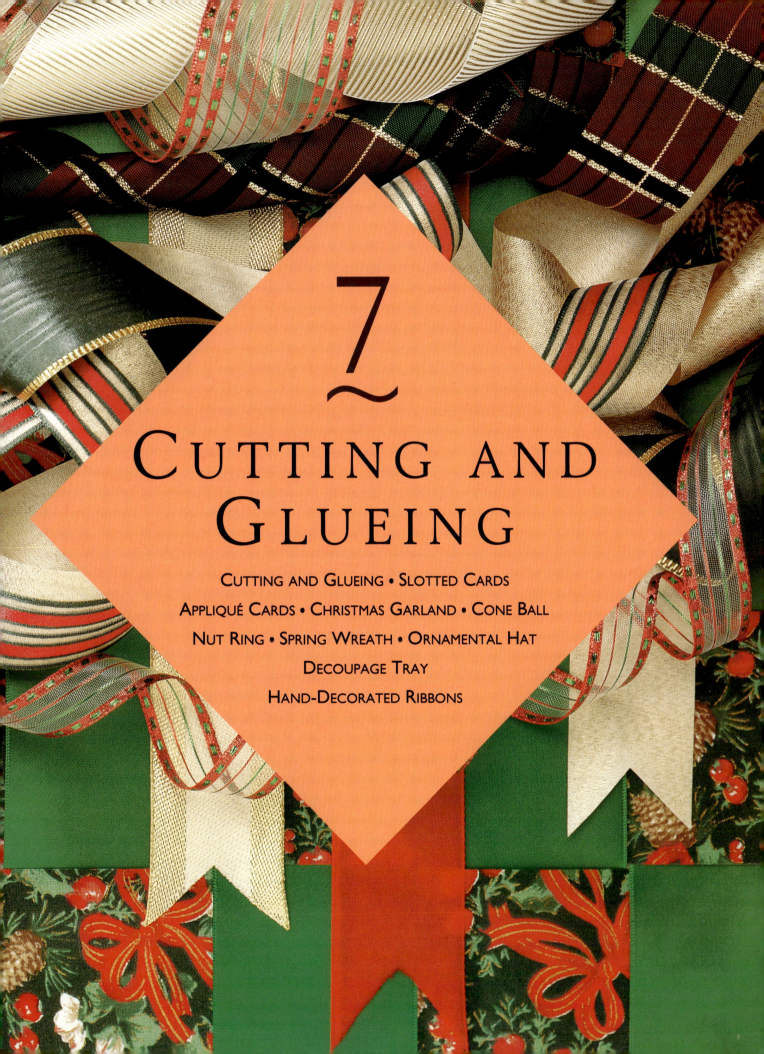

7

CUTTING AND GLUEING

CUTTING AND GLUEING • SLOTTED CARDS

APPLIQUÉ CARDS • CHRISTMAS GARLAND • CONE BALL

NUT RING • SPRING WREATH • ORNAMENTAL HAT

DECOUPAGE TRAY

HAND-DECORATED RIBBONS

CUTTING AND GLUEING

Craft (cut-edge) ribbons, available in a multitude of colours and finishes, are ideal for many decorative ribbon projects.

Craft ribbon can be used in the same way as woven-edge ribbon or it can be cut into shapes for making flowers and leaves or used for decoupage. This type of ribbon pleats beautifully and can be splayed into fan shapes.

variety of motifs and then move them around on your chosen surface until a design begins to "gel". Don't be afraid to overlap cuttings for effect, or to turn a motif into something different. For example, you could cut a large flower into the shape of an egg.

CRAFT RIBBONS

Craft ribbons and lace, which are treated with special finishes to curb fraying, are generally stiffer than woven-edge ribbons, making them ideal for loops and bows that need to maintain their shape as well as for a host of other craft projects.

Craft ribbons are not washable, so reserve them for projects such as cards and garlands that you don't want to keep forever.

DECOUPAGE

This is another craft for which these ribbons are ideal. Decoupage, whose name comes from the French word *couper*, to cut, was a very popular craft in Victorian times. All kinds of wooden surfaces were covered in cut-out illustrations, which were then given several layers of varnish.

Craft ribbons lend themselves perfectly to this hobby, as they are just as easy to cut and glue down as pieces of paper. If you use ribbons with a printed pattern you can cut a variety of motifs and borders, and the ribbon won't fray because of the special fabric finish.

The best way to work is to cut a

GLUE GUNS

These are very useful for projects where some bonding is required, such as greetings cards, decoupage items, decorated baskets and floral decorations. There are various different types on the market, some being "hot melt" and others "low melt". Whichever you choose always follow the manufacturer's instructions, and be sure to keep the gun out of the reach of children. Always hold the glued parts for several seconds to make sure the bond is strong.

A selection of pins in differing lengths are useful for securing roses and bows to displays.

Glue guns are ideal for bonding ribbons and dried flowers to wreaths and similar decorative items.

A variety of wires, both thick and thin, are essential for many craft projects involving cut and glued ribbon.

Fruits and berries are a clever way to introduce additional shape, colour and texture.

Wire cutters are a must for frequent users of stem and binding wires in craft projects.

FLORIST'S WIRE AND TAPE

A variety of wires and tapes are available from florists, gardening and craft shops and are used for various projects in this chapter. A sturdy but bendable wire is ideal for making stems for ribbon roses and bows and heavier dried flower heads and cones. This is often referred to as stem wire, and usually comes ready cut into lengths of between 15cm (6in) and 30cm (12in).

A finer wire is needed to fix a stem wire to the ribbon rose or other flower. It is also useful for securing the centres of bows and for attaching bows, roses and flowers and so on to floral wreaths, topiaries etc. Binding wire is made in a medium to fine gauge and is usually available by the reel.

Stemmed ribbon roses are enhanced with an artificial leaf or two. Smaller leaves are best with narrow ribbons.

Always cut craft wire with wire-cutters or old scissors, as it will ruin good fabric scissors.

You will also need florist's tape to bind wire stems and to attach leaves or other flowers. The wax tape sticks to itself and gives a smooth finish. It is sold by the reel and is usually green, although other colours are available in some stores.

A waxy, sticky tape for binding stems is available in green or brown.

A variety of bases are available for designing garlands, wreaths, posies and other arrange-ments.

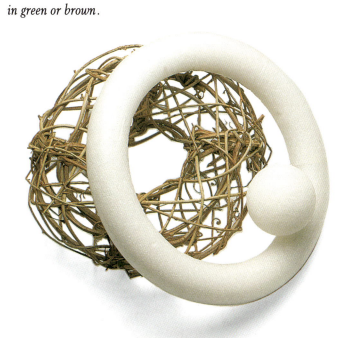

When using dried flowers as a general rule limit yourself to three colours excluding your main colour.

SLOTTED CARDS

A deceptively simple way to decorate a greetings card or gift tag, all you need is a craft knife, a cutting board, a ruler, pencil and glue.

CHRISTMAS TREE CARD AND GIFT TAG

MATERIALS

Craft ribbons – all 23mm (⅞in) wide
- 22cm (8¾in) green
- 8cm (3¼in) taffeta plaid
- 8cm (3¼in) red
- 4cm (1¾in) sheer
- 6cm (2¼in) light green
- 5cm (2in) swiss dot red

Doubleface satin ribbon – all 3mm (⅛in) wide
- 25cm (10in) mini-dot red
- 13cm (5in) white
- 1.40m (1½yd) red
- 40cm (15¾in) emerald green
- 13cm (5in) dark green

Other materials
- Piece of card 40.5cm by 16.5cm (16in by 6½in)
- Piece of card 27cm by 3.5cm (10½in by 1½in)
- Clear all-purpose adhesive

MAKING THE CARD

1 Score and fold the large piece of card into three as shown.

2 Trace the pattern onto the front section of the card, then cut the slots making sure they are cut cleanly to the edge.

3 Thread ribbon through slots, securing at the back with glue.

4 Thread the red 3mm (⅛in) ribbon in and out of the slots at the edges so that the longest pieces show on the front.

5 Tie bows at corners, glue tails into position, and glue first two folds of card together to finish.

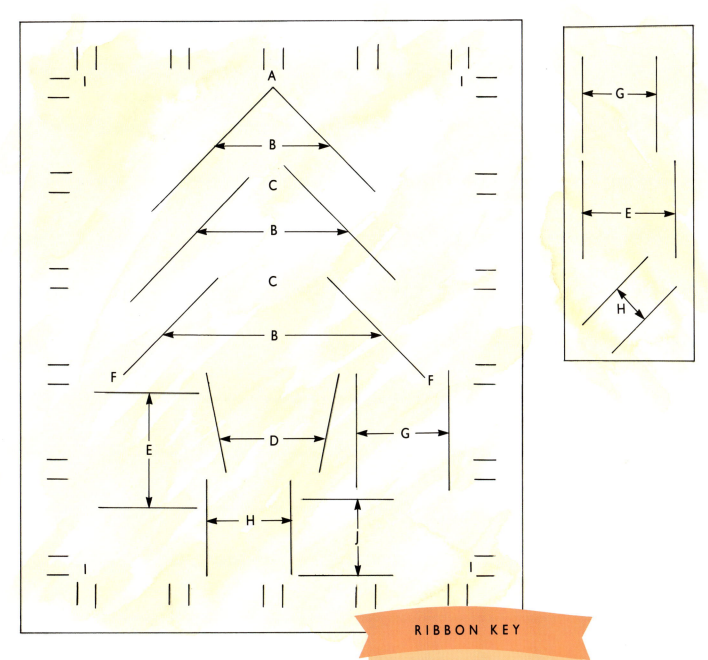

MAKING THE GIFT TAG

1 Score and fold remaining card into three 9cm (3½in) folds as before.

2 Cut slots, decorate with ribbon and finish as before.

RIBBON KEY

A = Silver star
B = Green and gold
C = Mini-dot red bow
D = Swiss dot red
E = Taffeta plaid
F = Emerald green bow
G = Red
H = Light green
I = Red bow
J = Sheer

METALLIC STAR

MAKING THE STAR

1 Enlarge the pattern opposite and trace it onto the navy card, then cut slots and thread ribbon horizontally.

2 Glue ends in place on reverse side and cut through ribbons at centre.

3 Fold and carefully glue each cut end back on itself to expose the other centre slots.

4 Thread vertical ribbons through, and glue ends in place on reverse side.

5 Score down centre of the white card and fold in half.

6 Mount navy card onto the front of white card and colour border with a gold pen.

MAKING THE GIFT TAG

1 Following pattern cut slots on blue card.

Scale 1 square = 8mm (⁵⁄₁₆in)

A panel of woven ribbon over which a window in the shape of your chosen design has been placed, is a quick way to make a pretty card. Zig-zag weave (above) makes an effective Christmas tree design.

2 Glue vertical pieces of ribbon in place as shown, then weave and glue the horizontal ribbons.
3 Mount the blue card on white card to finish.

For a three-dimensional effect, place wadding under your woven panel. The Valentine's Day card (right) also uses appliquéd lace ribbon to add to its romantic appeal.

APPLIQUÉ CARDS

Using highly versatile craft ribbon, individual handmade gift and greeting cards are fun to design and wonderful to receive, and need not be time-consuming to make.

WEDDING CARD AND GIFT TAG

MATERIALS

Ribbons
- 27cm (11in) of 56mm (2¼in) wide silver
- 1.50m (1¾yd) of 1.5mm (⅟₁₆in) wide white
- Four small ribbon roses

Other materials
- Square of net 12cm (4¾in)
- White card 18cm by 28cm (7in by 11in)
- Pale blue card 18cm by 14cm (7in by 5½in)
- Pale coloured paper 18cm by 14cm (7in by 5½in)
- White card 18cm by 28cm (7in by 11in)
- White card 11cm by 5.6cm (4½in by 2¼in) for the tag

MAKING THE CARD

1 Score down centre of white card and fold in half.

2 Stick the pale blue card over front of white card.

3 Cut out a 10cm (4in) square from the centre of the pale pastel paper to make a window.

4 Glue the net behind this window, then glue the paper window onto the blue card.

MAKING THE BELL

1 Trace the bell shape and make a template, then cut two bells from the wide silver craft ribbon.

2 Glue bells on net, glue on lace trim, and dress with three ribbon roses and about 1m (1¼yd) of white ribbon, following the photograph.

MAKING THE TAG

1 Cover the 11cm by 5.6cm (4½in by 2¼in) card with silver craft ribbon and fold in half.

2 Dress with white ribbon and a ribbon rose, punch a hole in the corner and thread with 13cm (5in) of white ribbon.

3 Make the half flowers in the same way, but after stitching and opening out the first fan, glue only from the centre to one outside edge, then adjust the pleats to form a semi-circle.

4 To make foliage curls cut eight 10cm (4in) lengths of the 9mm (⅜in) wide green ribbon. Roll each length tightly and glue at base to create four double curls.

MAKING THE CARD

1 Score down centre of 18cm by 36cm (7in by 14in) card and fold in half.

2 From the contrast card cut out centre to leave a 13mm (½in) border all round. Stick to front of card.

3 Glue four full flowers, three half flowers and three foliage curls in place.

MAKING THE TAG

1 Cover the 13cm by 3.9cm (5in by 1½in) card with craft ribbon.

2 Score card, fold in half and glue a half flower and foliage curl to the front, following the photograph.

3 Punch a hole in one corner, and thread with 13cm (5in) length of 1.5mm (¹⁄₁₆in) wide ribbon.

BIRTHDAY CARD AND GIFT TAG

MATERIALS

Ribbons
- 18cm (7in) of 39mm (1½in) wide craft in two different floral prints; 10cm (4in) in a third print
- 80cm (32in) of 9mm (⅜in) wide craft in pale green
- 13cm (5in) of 1.5mm (¹⁄₁₆in) wide blue ribbon

Other materials
- Card 18cm by 36cm (7in by 14in)
- Card 18cm (7in) square in contrasting colour
- Card 13cm by 3.9cm (5in by 1½in)
- Sewing thread

MAKING THE FLOWERS AND FOLIAGE

Using 39mm (1½in) wide craft ribbon, make four full and four half flowers as follows. Each full flower needs approximately 10cm (4in) of ribbon, and each half flower approximately 7cm (2¾in) of ribbon.

1 For the full flowers, fold the ribbon concertina-fashion every 7mm (¼in), stitch through centre, pull tight and secure.

2 Open out one side into a fan, glue end fold to the end fold of the other half, then open out other side; sew a sequin in centre.

CHRISTMAS WREATH
CARD AND TAG

MATERIALS

- 28cm (11in) of 32mm (1¼in) wide craft ribbon in Christmas colours
- Ribbon bow
- White card 18cm by 28cm (7in by 11in)
- Red card 18cm by 14cm (7in by 5½in)
- White card 13cm by 3.2cm (5in by 1¼in)
- Small piece of 32mm (1¼in) craft ribbon in colour to blend with bow
- 13cm (5in) of 1.5mm (¹⁄₁₆in) ribbon

MAKING THE CARD

1 Score down centre of white card and fold in half.

2 Cut a 10cm (4in) square window in middle of red card and glue to the white card.

3 Make 6mm (¼in) pleats in ribbon and stitch through near base.

4 Pull up thread and secure, then make into a circle by opening out pleats and glueing ends together.

5 Trim the pleated circle with a bow, then glue it within the frame.

MAKING THE TAG

1 Cover one side of the card with craft ribbon.

2 Score and fold card down centre, cutting a V in the ends of the card to look like bow tails.

3 Punch a hole in corner of the card and thread with the 1.5mm (¹⁄₁₆in) ribbon.

CHRISTMAS GARLAND

Traditional tartans, stripes and festive green and red ribbons are the basis for this sumptuous garland, ideal for placing along a mantelpiece or bannister rail.

Ribbons
- 1.50m (1¾yd) of 39mm (1½in) wide cut-edge green velour
- 1.50 (1¾yd) of 39mm (1½in) wide tartan
- 2.90m (3¼yd) of 39mm (1½in) wide red/green/gold
- 5m (5½yd) of 23mm (⅞in) wide tartan

Other materials
- 1.30m (1½yd) twisted vine
- 4m (4⅓yd) gold beading
- Eight small sprays artificial berries
- Twenty pine cones sprayed gold
- Florist's stub wire and glue

MAKING THE GARLAND

1 Cut the cut-edge red/green/gold into two 70cm (27in) lengths. Cut each piece lengthwise into three and make six multiloop bows (see page 86) mounted on florist's stub wire.

2 From the 23mm (⅞in) tartan cut-edge make ten multiloop bows mounted on florist's wire.

3 Mount the sprayed pine cones on stub wire and bind the gold beading around the whole length of the vine.

4 Mark the centre point of the vine and arrange all the berries, cones and bows along the length, pushing the wires into the vine and glueing to secure.

5 Make three large multiloop bows with tails from three 1.50m (1¾yd) lengths of the 39mm (1½in) wide ribbon, and put them together to form one large bow.

6 Position this bow in the centre of the vine, glue in place, and trim tails to desired length.

CONE BALL

Pretty enough to use singly, or in a group, decorated cone balls look attractive suspended from the ceiling at different heights, rather like chime bells.

MAKING THE BALL

1 Pierce the foam ball through its centre with the stub wire, bending each end to form a small loop close to the ball. Trim off any excess.

2 Cut two 20cm (8in) lengths of the 23mm (⅞in) wide sand ribbon and use binding wire to make two double loops.

3 Make six stitched ribbon roses (see page 97) with the remaining sand ribbon, and another two loops and six roses from the 23mm (⅞in) wide light brown ribbon.

4 Cut six 15cm (6in) lengths of gold ribbon and use binding wire to make six double loops.

5 From the remaining gold ribbon make three stitched ribbon roses.

6 Set aside two 60cm (24in) lengths of 15mm (⅝in) wide satin print ribbon, then use wire to make fourteen double loops from the remaining printed ribbon.

MATERIALS

Ribbons
- 1.80m (2yd) of 23mm (⅞in) satin sand
- 2.25m (2½yd) of 15mm (⅝in) wide satin gold
- 1.80m (2yd) of 23mm (⅞in) wide acetate light brown
- 60cm (24in) of 15mm (⅝in) wide acetate light brown
- 3.40m (4yd) of 15mm (⅝in) wide satin print

Other materials
- Dry foam ball 10cm (4in) diameter
- About thirty-six small pine cones, varnished or painted
- Binding wire
- 15cm (6in) length of stub wire
- Clear all-purpose adhesive

7 Make four wired double loops from the light brown 15mm (⅝in) wide ribbon.

8 Thread one 60cm (24in) length of printed ribbon through the wire loop on one side of the ball, and stitch or knot the ends together to form a hanging loop.

9 Thread the remaining printed ribbon and gold ribbon together through the opposite stub wire loop to form the lower tail.

10 Cover the ball with prepared roses, loops and cones, pinning or glueing them in place.

NUT RING

For a delightful centrepiece for the Christmas table, make a traditional nut ring and add colourful ribbons to contrast with the natural dark brown tones.

MAKING THE RING

1 Divide the nuts, pods and cones into four equal groups.

2 At the 3, 6, 9 and 12 o'clock positions on the ring, wire or glue the groups of nuts, pods and cones, leaving a gap of 5cm (2in) between the adjacent groups; spray with varnish.

3 Cut four 7.5cm (3in) lengths of velvet ribbon. Fishtail one end of each piece and make a pleat and stitch in place at the other.

4 Glue the stitched end flat to the ring between each group of nuts with the "fishtail" protruding outwards.

MATERIALS

Ribbons
- 60cm (24in) of 68mm (2¾in) wide velvet burgundy
- 3.90m (4yd) of 39mm (1½in) wide plaid
- 1.80m (2yd) of 23mm (⅞in) wide metallic nylon copper

Other materials
- Vine ring approx 23cm (9in) diameter
- 450gm (1lb) of assorted nuts
- Eight jacaranda pods
- Four larch cones
- Twelve macrocarpa cones
- Binding wire
- Clear varnish
- Clear all-purpose adhesive

5 Cut the plaid ribbon into four, fold and wire each piece into a treble folded bow, fishtail the ends and glue or wire on top of each velvet tail.

6 Cut the metallic ribbon into four, fold and wire each one into a double folded bow, cut the ends at a slant, glue or wire one to the side of each plaid bow.

7 Cut four pieces of velvet ribbon 7.5cm (3in) long and cut them all in half lengthwise. Fishtail one end of each piece and stitch a pleat at the other. Glue two tails between the loops of each plaid bow.

SPRING WREATH

Celebrate spring with a birch wreath decorated with bright coloured ribbons and flowers. Suspend it from a ceiling or, without hanging ribbons, on a door or wall.

MATERIALS

Ribbons
- 6m (6½yd) of 23mm (⅞in) wide yellow
- 4.50m (5yd) of 23mm (⅞in) wide wire-edge, pale yellow

Other materials
- Twisted birch or cane wreath
- Dried flowers and grasses

MAKING THE WREATH

1 Cut the satin ribbon in half. Make the hanging ribbons by cutting one 3m (3¼yd) piece into three equal lengths and attaching them at equal spaces to the wreath.

2 Glue the flowers and grasses around the wreath.

3 Using the wire-edge ribbon, make three multiloop bows (see page 86), and glue one at the base of each hanging ribbon.

4 From the remaining singleface satin ribbon, make a multiloop satin bow and glue to the wreath below the point where the hanging ribbon is attached.

ORNAMENTAL HAT

Bring back memories of sunny summer days with a decorative straw hat to hang on the wall. Select your ribbons and dried flowers to complement your room.

MAKING THE DECORATIONS

1 Make ten multiloop bows (see page 86) from the lace ribbon, nine from the gingham, three from 1.80m (2yd) of cut-edge floral ribbon, and one large multiloop bow with tails from the remaining floral ribbon.

2 Attach a short length of ribbon or string inside the hat for hanging.

3 Place hat flat on a table and glue all the pieces in place, fixing the large multiloop bow to the bottom of the hat, with a small gingham bow in the centre.

MATERIALS

Ribbons
- 5m (5½yd) of 15mm (⅝in) wide lace
- 4.50m (5yd) of 15mm (⅝in) wide gingham
- 4m (4⅓yd) of 39mm (1½in) wide cut-edge floral

Other materials
- Large straw hat
- Assorted dried flowers, grasses and artificial flower sprays
- Small piece of ribbon or string

Decoupage Tray

Craft ribbons lend themselves well to decoupage; you can cut a variety of borders and motifs, and the ribbon won't fray because of the special fabric finish.

1 Prepare the surface of the tray by either stripping off existing varnish or painting the central panel. You need a clean grease-free surface for the decoupage.

2 Cut the pieces of border ribbon to fit, and glue them on, leaving a small margin at the outer edges.

3 Carefully cut out motifs and shapes that appeal to you and arrange them on the tray. Cut out flowers singly, and overlap your cuttings for an interesting effect.

4 When you are satisfied with your design, glue the shapes into place.

5 Use masking tape to mask any areas that you need to protect from varnish, such as the edges of the tray, then apply a thin coat of varnish and leave to dry.

6 Continue to apply further thin coats of varnish, leaving each one to dry first, until the cuttings have a

MATERIALS

- Craft ribbon – sufficient wide print with repeating pattern to make a border, plus floral prints for individual motifs
- Paper glue
- Wooden tray
- Paint and brushes
- Clear polyurethane varnish
- Sandpaper

glazed appearance. You will need about 15 coats.

7 Rub down the varnish with fine sandpaper, wipe off the dust and apply the final coat of varnish, then remove any masking tape, using a knife to free the edges if necessary.

HAND-DECORATED RIBBONS

*Customize accessories for home, work and school
by embellishing ribbons with fabric paints, beads,
sequins, stencils and other decorative findings.*

*Create your own
fireworks with
interesting
combinations of
glitter paints, gold
paint and plastic
paint.*

FABRIC PAINTS

There are many types of fabric paint available giving a variety of surface effects: raised or flat, shiny, glittery, matt or metallic. Try splattering paint on ribbon, or apply a stencil using a special stubby stencil brush. Stencils look best on smooth satins in light colours to make lovely trims for home furnishings. Paint ribbons on a flat surface before making them into bows etc. Experiment techniques on spare ribbon first, follow manufacturers' instructions carefully, and always test for colour-fastness for use on washable items.

BEADS, PEARLS, SEQUINS, BUTTONS

Decorative jewellery findings, sequins and buttons look superb on ribbon. Either handstitch them or choose a fabric paint which doubles as a glue. Decorate bows or rosettes after you have made them and choose small, lightweight embellishments so the ribbon is not weighed down. Washing can damage the beads or they might come off altogether, so make sure that ribbon can be removed for laundering if necessary.

SPRAY PAINTING

For a completely co-ordinated look make bows and roses in any left-over ribbons to create a table arrangement or tree decoration along with baubles and artificial or dried flowers, then give the whole lot a couple of coats of spray paint.

Gold, silver or bronze works well for Christmas, and as the paint stiffens the ribbon, even a single rose or bow in a fine sheer ribbon makes a dramatic and unusual trim for a parcel or Christmas tree.

*Use a paint brush
and add a touch of
water to the fabric
paint to produce an
artistic
watercolour effect.*

*Generally the more
dilute the paint,
the softer the
finished texture.*

Painted musical notes on polka dot ribbon and hearts and flowers on houndstooth checks provide a light-hearted statement.

The appearance of plastic paint varies according to the type of ribbon you choose. Simple swirls and dots on a gold and black jacquard gives surface texture. Hieroglyphics look dramatic in black on bright coloured ribbon.

Whether you choose plain satins, dots, plaids, stripes or moiré taffeta, painting on ribbon knows no bounds. Using a variety of colours, write your name, do your sums or write the alphabet.

A glitter paint pen has been used to draw around the outline of a pretty floral printed ribbon (left). This technique can be used to highlight interesting motifs and details.

Plastic-look fabric paint (above) is available in primary fluorescent glitter or pearlized colours and is great for creating surface texture. To attach sequins, beads, bows or diamanté, just squeeze a blob from the bottle and place the item gently on the paint.

Create all kinds of pop art effects and enjoy the freedom of paint experimentation on ribbon (below). The golden rule is to keep the design simple.

Gold fabric paint produces a rich, oriental look (left).

INDEX

Page references in *italic* type refer to pictures and captions.

A

appliqué techniques, 62-3
    cards, 114-6

B

back stitch, 33
bags
    appliquéd evening bag, 72
    child's bag, 74
    make-up, 40
barrel cushion, 22
baskets
    Christmas, 92
    Easter, 93
    embroidery motif, 40
beads, decorating ribbons with, 123
bed linen, appliquéd, *64*
bell shape, 114
belts, 71
binding wire, 109
birthday card, 115
bows, 82-6
    basic loop, 83
    centre-bound, 83
    Christmas decorations, 90-1
    double, 83
    embellishments for, 123
    for fan rosette centre, 54
    florist's, 86
    for gift wraps, 88-9
    hand-tied, 82
    layered, 84
    looped on card, 84
    multiloop, 86
    picture bow, 87
    pompon, 85
box pleat, 51
bridal head-dress, 100
bride's bouquet, 101
bridesmaid's rose ball, 102
buttons
    decorating with, 123
    folded button, 52

C

cards
    appliqué, 114-16
    birthday, 115
    Christmas, 110, 112, 116
    slotted, 110-13
    Valentine, *113*
    wedding, 36, 144
casings, 63
Catherine wheel rosette, 56
    on felt hat, 58
centre-bound bow, 83
chain stitch, 33
child's dress and bag, 74
christening card, flower motif for, *45*
Christmas decorations
    basket, 92
    bows, 90-1
    cards, 110, 112, 116
    cone ball, 118
    garland, 117
    gift tags, 111, 112, 116
    nut ring, 119
    spray painting, 123
    table linen, 38
coaster, 21
cone ball, 118
corsage, *99*, *101*
couching, 33
Courthouse Steps, 63
craft (cut-edge, florist's) ribbons, 9, 108
Cretan stitch, 33
curtain tie-backs, 78
cushions
    barrel, 22
    embroidered, 45
    frilled, 65
    piped, 66
    trims, 76-7
cut-edge ribbons, *see* craft ribbons
cutting and glueing, 108

D

daisy rosette, 53
decoupage, 108
    tray, 122

double bow, 83
double feather stitch, 32
dress, child's, 74

E

Easter basket, 93
edgings, applying, 63
embellished ribbons, 13
embroidery techniques and stitches, 32-3
    back stitch, 33
    chain stitch, 33
    couching, 33
    Cretan stitch, 33
    double feather stitch, 32
    feather stitch, 32
    fishbone, 33
    fly stitch, 33
    French knot, 33
    herringbone stitch, 33
    lazy daisy stitch, 33
    running stitch, 33
    stem stitch, 33
evening bag, 72

F

fan rosette, 54
feather stitch, 32
    double, 32
fishbone stitch, 33
five-strand braid, 50
florette rosette, 55
florist's bow, 85
florist's ribbons *see* craft ribbons
florist's tape, 109
florist's wire, 109
flowers, dried
    pot pourri sachets, 57
    restricting colours, *109*
    Spring wreath, 120
flowers, fresh, 86
    lavender, *20*
flowers, ribbon
    embroidered basket, 40
    embroidered, for cushion, 46
    folded and glued, 115

fly stitch, 33
folding
    folded button, 52
    folded plait, 50
foliage
    embroided loop leaves, 47
    glued curls, 115
    frame, picture, 34
    French knot, 33

G

garland, Christmas, 117
gathering, 52
    pre-gathered ribbons, 13
gift tags
    birthday, 115
    Christmas, 111, 112, 116
    wedding, 114
gift wrapping
    bows for, 88-9
    rose-trimmed parcels, 104-5
glueing, 108
    glue guns, 108
grosgrain ribbons, 10

H

hair decorations
    florette rosette, 55
    looped bows, 84
hand-decorating, 123-5
hand-tied bow, 82
hat decorations
    felt-hat with Catherine wheel
        rosette, 58
    felt hat with lily rosette, 58
    florette rosette, 55
    ornamental hat, 121
    velvet hat with semi-circular
        rosette, 59
    wedding hat, 58
herringbone stitch, 33

I

interfacing
    preparing for weaving, 16
    using for large number of ribbons, 62
iridescent ribbons, 12

J

jacquard ribbons, 11

L

lavender in ribbon, *20*
layered bow, 84
lazy daisy stitch, 33
leaves *see* foliage
lily rosette, 53
    on felt hat, 58
    flat, 53
Log Cabin Patchwork, 62
log cabin quilt, 68
loop bow, basic, 83
loop braid, 50
looped bow on card, 84
loops in rosettes, 54

M

make-up bag, 40
merrowed craft ribbons, 9
metallic ribbons, 12
metric conversion chart, 13
Missouri Puzzle, 62
mitring, 63
monofilament-edge ribbons, 12
multiloop bow, 86
    for gift-wrapping, 88-9

N

nail block (for bow-making), 82
napkin ring, *103*
napkins, Christmas, 38
nut ring centrepiece, 119

O

ombré taffeta ribbons, 11

P

paints for ribbons, 123
parcels *see* gift wrapping
patchwork designs, 62-3
    Courthouse Steps, 63
    Log Cabin, 62
    Missouri Puzzle, 62
    Pineapple, 63
    String Quilted Diamond, 62
patchwork weave, 18
petal rosette, 55
pictures
    bow decoration for, 87
    frame, 34
    sampler, 42

Pineapple (patchwork design), 63
plain weave square, 17
plaiting, 50
    five-strand braid, 50
    folded plait, 50
    loop braid, 50
    simple plait, 50
pleating, 51
    box pleat, 51
    pre-pleated ribbons, 13
    simple pleat, 51
pompon bow, 85
pot pourri sachets, 57
pre-pleated ribbons, 13
pregathered ribbons, 13

Q

quantities
    for appliqué and patchwork, 62
    estimating for weaves, 16
    for roses and rosebuds, 96
quilt
    log cabin, 68
    woven-square, 24

R

roses and rosebuds, 96-8
    quantities and widths, 96
    ribbon rosette, 98
    stemmed rose, 96
    stitched rose, 97
    tension, 96
    wire-edge ribbon rose, 98
rosettes, 53-6
    Catherine wheel, 56
    embellishments for, 123
    fan, 54
    florette, 55
    petal, 55
        for barrel cushion, 23
    ribbon daisy, 53
    ribbon lily, 53
        flat, 53
    ribbon rose, 98
    semi-circular, 59
running stitch, 33

S

sachets, pot pourri, 57
sampler, 42
satin ribbons, 10
    embellished, 13